THE
ELEMENTS
OF
PROGRAMMING
STYLE

THE
ELEMENTS
OF
PROGRAMMING
STYLE

Second Edition

Brian W. Kernighan

Bell Laboratories
Murray Hill, New Jersey

P. J. Plauger

Yourdon, Inc.
New York, New York

McGRAW-HILL BOOK COMPANY

New York   St. Louis   San Francisco   Auckland   Bogotá   Düsseldorf
Johannesburg   London   Madrid   Mexico   Montreal   New Delhi
Panama   Paris   São Paulo   Singapore   Sydney   Tokyo   Toronto

Library of Congress Cataloging in Publication Data

Kernighan, Brian W.
  The elements of programming style.

  Bibliography: p.
  Includes index.
  1. Electronic digital computers—Programming.
I. Plauger, P.J., date   joint author.
II. Title.
QA76.6.K47 1978   001.6'42   78-3498
ISBN 0-07-034207-5

The Elements of Programming Style

234567890 DODO 78321098

This book was set in Times Roman and Courier 12 by the authors, using a Graphic Systems phototypesetter driven by a PDP-11/70 running under the UNIX operating system.

UNIX is a Trademark of Bell Laboratories.

We are deeply indebted to the following authors and publishers for their kind permission to reproduce excerpts from the following copyrighted material:

R. V. Andree, J. P. Andree, and D. D. Andree, *Computer Programming Techniques, Analysis, and Mathematics*. Copyright © 1973 by R. V. Andree. By permission of Prentice-Hall, Inc.

F. Bates and M. L. Douglas, *Programming Language/One with Structured Programming (Third Edition)*. Copyright © 1975 by Prentice-Hall, Inc. Reprinted by permission.

C. R. Bauer and A. P. Peluso, *Basic Fortran IV with Watfor & Watfiv*. Copyright © 1974 by Addison-Wesley Publishing Company, Inc. By permission.

C. R. Bauer, A. P. Peluso, and D. A. Gomberg, *Basic PL/I Programming*. Copyright © 1968 by Addison-Wesley Publishing Company, Inc. By permission.

M. Bohl and A. Walter, *Introduction to PL/I Programming and PL/C*. Copyright © 1973 by Science Research Associates, Inc. Reprinted by permission of the publisher.

V. J. Calderbank, *A Course on Programming in Fortran IV*. Copyright © 1969 by Chapman and Hall, Ltd. By permission.

Paul M. Chirlian, *Introduction to Fortran IV*. Copyright © 1973 by Academic Press. By permission.

Frank J. Clark, *Introduction to PL/I Programming*. Copyright © 1971 by Allyn and Bacon, Inc. By permission.

Computerworld. Copyright © 1972 by *Computerworld*, Newton, Mass. 02160. By permission.

Datamation®. Copyright © 1972, 1973 by Technical Publishing Company, Greenwich, Connecticut 06830. Reprinted with permission.

D. F. DeTar, *Principles of Fortran Programming*. Copyright © 1972 by W. A. Benjamin, Inc., Menlo Park, California. By permission of the publisher.

H. Dinter, *Introduction to Computing*. Copyright © 1973, Heinz Dinter. By permission of The Macmillan Company, New York.

D. Dmitry and T. Mott, Jr., *Introduction to Fortran IV Programming*. Copyright © Holt, Rinehart and Winston, Inc., 1966. By permission.

V. T. Dock, *Fortran IV Programming*, Copyright © 1972 by Reston Publishing Company, Inc. By permission.

W. S. Dorn, G. G. Bitter, and D. L. Hector, *Computer Applications for Calculus*. Copyright © Prindle, Weber & Schmidt, Inc., 1972. By permission.

W. S. Dorn and D. D. McCracken, *Numerical Methods with Fortran IV Case Studies*. Copyright © 1972 by John Wiley & Sons, Inc. By permission.

L. E. Edwards, *PL/I for Business Applications*. Copyright © 1973 by Reston Publishing Company, Inc. By permission.

M. V. Farina, *Fortran IV Self-Taught*. Copyright © Prentice-Hall, Inc., 1966. By permission.

B. S. Gottfried, *Programming with Fortran IV*. Copyright © 1972 by Quantum Publishers, Inc. By permission.

Gabriel F. Groner, *PL/I Programming in Technological Applications*. Copyright © 1971 by John Wiley and Sons, Inc. Reprinted by permission of the publisher.

J. N. Haag, *Comprehensive Standard Fortran Programming*. Copyright © Hayden Book Company, Inc., 1969. By permission.

J. K. Hughes, *PL/I Programming*. Copyright © 1973 by John Wiley & Sons, Inc. By permission.

J. K. Hughes and J. I. Michtom, *A Structured Approach to Programming*. Copyright © 1977 by Prentice-Hall, Inc. Reprinted by permission.

R. J. Kochenburger and C. J. Turcio, *Introduction to PL/I and PL/C Programming - Instructor's Guide*. Copyright © 1974 by John Wiley & Sons, Inc. By permission.

C. B. Kreitzberg and B. Shneiderman, *The Elements of Fortran Style*. Copyright © 1972 by Harcourt Brace Jovanovich, Inc. By permission.

J. L. Kuester and J. H. Mize, *Optimization Techniques with Fortran*. Copyright © 1973 by McGraw-Hill, Inc. By permission.

S. S. Kuo, *Computer Applications of Numerical Methods*. Copyright © Addison-Wesley Publishing Company, 1972. By permission.

H. L. Ledgard, *Programming Proverbs*. Copyright © 1975 by Hayden Book Company. By permission.

R. S. Ledley, *Fortran IV Programming*. Copyright © McGraw-Hill, Inc., 1966. By permission.

G. O. Manifold, *Calculating With Fortran*. Copyright © 1972 by Charles E. Merrill Publishing Co., Inc. By permission.

W. A. Manning and R. S. Garnero, *A Fortran IV Problem Solver*. Copyright © McGraw-Hill, Inc., 1970. By permission.

E. Marxer and D. Hartford, *Elements of Computer Programming: Fortran*. Copyright © 1973. Published by Delmar Publishers, a division of Litton Educational Publishing, Inc. By permission.

D. D. McCracken, *A Guide to Fortran IV Programming*. Copyright © 1965 by John Wiley and Sons, Inc. Reprinted by permission of the publisher.

CONTENTS

PREFACE to the Second Edition

The practice of computer programming has changed since *The Elements of Programming Style* first appeared. Programming style has become a legitimate topic of discussion. After years of producing "write-only code," students, teachers, and computing professionals now recognize the importance of readable programs. There has also been a widespread acceptance of structured programming as a valuable coding discipline, and a growing recognition that program design is an important phase, too often neglected in the past.

We have revised *The Elements of Programming Style* extensively to reflect these changes. The first edition avoided any direct mention of the term "structured programming," to steer well clear of the religious debates then prevalent. Now that the fervor has subsided, we feel comfortable in discussing structured coding techniques that actually work well in practice.

The second edition devotes a whole new chapter to program structure, showing how top-down design can lead to better organized programs. Design issues are discussed throughout the text. We have made considerable use of pseudo-code as a program development tool.

We have also rewritten many of the examples presented in the first edition, to reflect (we hope) a greater understanding of how to program well. There are new examples as well, including several from the first edition which now serve as models of how *not* to do things. New exercises have been added. Finally, we have extended and generalized our rules of good style.

We are once again indebted to the authors and publishers who have graciously given us permission to reprint material from their textbooks. Looking back on some of our own examples makes us realize how demanding an effort good programming is.

We would also like to thank friends who read the second edition in draft form. In particular, Al Aho, Jim Blue, Stu Feldman, Paul Kernighan, Doug McIlroy, Ralph Muha, and Dick Wexelblat provided us with valuable suggestions.

Brian W. Kernighan

P. J. Plauger

PREFACE to the First Edition

Good programming cannot be taught by preaching generalities. The way to learn to program well is by seeing, over and over, how real programs can be improved by the application of a few principles of good practice and a little common sense. Practice in critical reading leads to skill in rewriting, which in turn leads to better writing.

This book is a study of a large number of "real" programs, each of which provides one or more lessons in style. We discuss the shortcomings of each example, rewrite it in a better way, then draw a general rule from the specific case. The approach is pragmatic and down-to-earth; we are more interested in improving current programming practice than in setting up an elaborate theory of how programming should be done. Consequently, this book can be used as a supplement in a programming course at any level, or as a refresher for experienced programmers.

The examples we give are all in Fortran and PL/I, since these languages are widely used and are sufficiently similar that a reading knowledge of one means that the other can also be *read* well enough. (We avoid complicated constructions in either language and explain unavoidable idioms as we encounter them.) *The principles of style, however, are applicable in all languages, including assembly codes.*

Our aim is to teach the elements of good style in a small space, so we concentrate on essentials. Rules are laid down throughout the text to emphasize the lessons learned. Each chapter ends with a summary and a set of "points to ponder," which provide exercises and a chance to investigate topics not fully covered in the text itself. Finally we collect our rules in one place for handy reference.

A word on the sources of the examples: *all* of the programs we use are taken from programming textbooks. Thus, we do not set up artificial programs to illustrate our points — we use finished products, written and published by experienced programmers. Since these examples are typically the first code seen by a novice programmer, we would hope that they would be models of good style. Unfortunately, we sometimes find that the opposite is true — textbook examples often demonstrate the state of the art of computer programming all too well. (We have done our best to play fair — we don't think that any of the programs are made to look bad by being quoted out of context.)

Let us state clearly, however, that we intend no criticism of textbook authors, either individually or as a class. Shortcomings show only that we are all human, and that under the pressure of a large, intellectually demanding task like writing a program or a book, it is much too easy to do some things imperfectly. We have no doubt that a few of our "good" programs will provide "bad" examples for some future writer — we hope only that he and his readers will learn from the experience of studying them carefully.

A manual of programming style could not have been written without the pioneering work of numerous people, many of whom have written excellent programming textbooks. D. D. McCracken and G. M. Weinberg, for instance, have long taught the virtues of simplicity and clarity. And the work of E. W. Dijkstra and Harlan Mills on structured programming has made possible our rules for properly specifying flow of control. The form and approach of this book has been strongly influenced by *The Elements of Style* by W. Strunk and E. B. White. We have tried to emulate their brevity by concentrating on the essential practical aspects of style.

We are indebted to many people for their help and encouragement. We would like especially to thank the authors and publishers who gave us permission to reproduce the computer programs used in this text. Their cooperation is greatly appreciated.

Our friends and colleagues at Bell Laboratories provided numerous useful suggestions, which we have incorporated, and saved us from more than one embarrassing blunder, which we have deleted. In particular, V. A. Vyssotsky bore with us through several revisions; for his perceptive comments and enthusiastic support at every stage of this book's evolution (and for several aphorisms we have shamelessly stolen) we are deeply grateful. We would also like to single out A. V. Aho, M. E. Lesk, M. D. McIlroy, and J. S. Thompson for the extensive time and assistance they gave to this project.

We were able to type the manuscript directly into a PDP 11/45, edit the source, check the programs, and set the final version in type — all with the help of a uniquely flexible operating system called UNIX. K. L. Thompson and D. M. Ritchie were the principal architects of UNIX; besides reading drafts, they helped us get the most out of the system while we were working on this book. J. F. Ossanna wrote the typesetting program and made several modifications for our special needs. We thank them.

Brian W. Kernighan

P. J. Plauger

THE
ELEMENTS
OF
PROGRAMMING
STYLE

Consider the program fragment

```
      DO 14 I=1,N
      DO 14 J=1,N
   14 V(I,J)=(I/J)*(J/I)
```

A modest familiarity with Fortran tells us that this doubly nested DO loop assigns something to each element of an N by N matrix V. What are the values assigned? I and J are positive integer variables and, in Fortran, integer division truncates toward zero. Thus when I is less than J, (I/J) is zero; conversely, when J is less than I, (J/I) is zero. When I equals J, both factors are one. So (I/J)*(J/I) is one if and only if I equals J; otherwise it is zero. The program fragment puts ones on the diagonal of V and zeros everywhere else. (V becomes an identity matrix.) How clever!

Or is it?

Suppose you encountered this fragment in a larger program. If your knowledge of Fortran is sufficiently deep, you may have enjoyed the clever use of integer division. Possibly you were appalled that two divisions, a multiplication, and a conversion from integer to floating point were invoked when simpler mechanisms are available. More likely, you were driven to duplicating the reasoning we gave above to understand what is happening. Far more likely, you formed a vague notion that something useful is being put into an array and simply moved on. Only if motivated strongly, perhaps by the need to debug or to alter the program, would you be likely to go back and puzzle out the precise meaning.

A better version of the fragment is

```
C  MAKE V AN IDENTITY MATRIX
      DO 14 I = 1,N
         DO 12 J = 1,N
   12       V(I,J) = 0.0
   14    V(I,I) = 1.0
```

This zeros each row, then changes its diagonal element to one. The intent is now reasonably clear, and the code even happens to execute faster. Had we been programming in PL/I, we could have been more explicit:

1

```
/* MAKE V AN IDENTITY MATRIX */
    V = 0.0;
    DO I = 1 TO N;
       V(I,I) = 1.0;
    END;
```

In either case, it is more important to make the purpose of the code unmistakable than to display virtuosity. Even storage requirements and execution time are unimportant by comparison, for setting up an identity matrix must surely be but a small part of the whole program. The problem with obscure code is that debugging and modification become much more difficult, and these are already the hardest aspects of computer programming. Besides, there is the added danger that a too-clever program may not say what you thought it said.

Write clearly — don't be too clever.

Let's pause for a moment and look at what we've done. We studied part of a program, taken verbatim from a programming textbook, and discussed what was good about it and what was bad. Then we made it better. (Not necessarily perfect — just better.) And then we drew a rule or a general conclusion from our analysis and improvements, a rule that would have sounded like a sweeping generality in the abstract, but which makes sense and can be applied once you've seen a specific case.

The rest of the book will be much the same thing — an example from a text, discussion, improvements, and a rule, repeated over and over. When you have finished reading the book, you should be able to criticize your own code. More important, you should be able to write it better in the first place, with less need for criticism.

We have tried to sort the examples into a logical progression, but as you shall see, real programs are like prose — they often violate simultaneously a number of rules of good practice. Thus our classification scheme may sometimes seem arbitrary and we will often have to digress.

Most of the examples will be bigger than the one we just saw, but not excessively so; with the help of our discussion, you should be able to follow them even if you're a beginner. In fact, most of the bigger programs will shrink before your very eyes as we modify them. Sheer size is often an illusion, reflecting only a need for improvement.

The examples are all in either Fortran or PL/I, but if one or both of these languages is unfamiliar, that shouldn't intimidate you any more than size should. Although you may not be able to write a PL/I program, say, you will certainly be able to read one well enough to understand the point we are making, and the practice in reading will make learning PL/I that much easier.

For example, here is a small part of a PL/I program that we will discuss in detail in Chapter 4:

```
        IF CTR > 45 THEN GO TO OVFLO;
        ELSE GO TO RDCARD;
OVFLO:
   ...
```

The first GOTO simply goes around the second GOTO, which seems a bit disorganized. If we replace > by <=, we can write

```
        IF CTR <= 45 THEN GOTO RDCARD;
OVFLO:
   ...
```

One less statement, simpler logic, and, as it happens, we no longer need the label OVFLO. The lesson? Don't branch around branches: turn relational tests around if it makes the program easier to understand. We will soon see a Fortran example of exactly the same failing, which brings up an important point: although details vary from language to language, *the principles of style are the same.* Branching around branches is confusing in any language. So even though you program in Cobol or Basic or assembly language or whatever, the guidelines you find here still apply.

It might seem that we're making a great fuss about a little thing in this last example. After all, it's still pretty obvious what the code says. The trouble is, although any single weakness causes no great harm, the cumulative effect of several confusing statements is code that is simply unintelligible.

Our next example is somewhat larger:

The following is a typical program to evaluate the square root (B) *of a number* (X):

```
        READ(5,1)X
    1   FORMAT(F10.5)
        A=X/2
    2   B=(X/A+A)/2
        C=B-A
        IF(C.LT.0)C=-C
        IF(C.LT.10.E-6)GOTO 3
        A=B
        GOTO 2
    3   WRITE(6,1)B
        STOP
        END
```

Because it is bigger, we can study it on several levels and learn something from each. For instance, before we analyze the code in detail, we might consider whether this program is truly "typical." It is unlikely that a square root routine would be packaged as a main program that reads its input from a file — a function with an argument would be far more useful. Even assuming that we really do want a main program that computes square roots, is it likely that we would want it to compute only one before stopping?

This unfortunate tendency to write overly restricted code influences how we write programs that are supposed to be general. Soon enough we shall meet programs designed to keep track of exactly seventeen salesmen, to sort precisely 500 numbers, to trace through just one maze. We can only guess at how much of the program rewriting that goes on every day actually amounts to entering parameters via the compiler.

Let us continue with the square root program. It is an implementation of Newton's method, which is indeed at the heart of many a library square root routine (although we need not go into precisely how it works). With proper data, the method converges rapidly. If X is negative, however, this program can go into an infinite loop. (Try it.) A good routine would instead provide an error return or a diagnostic message. And the program blows up in statement 2 if X is zero, a case that must be treated separately. The square root of zero should be reported as zero.

Even for strictly positive values of X this program can give garbage for an answer. The problem lies in the convergence test used:

```
C=B-A
IF(C.LT.0)C=-C
IF(C.LT.10.E-6)GOTO 3
```

To make effective use of the Fortran language, the second line should read

```
C = ABS(C)
```

To avoid having someone misread 10.E-6 as "10 to the minus sixth power," the constant in the third line should be 1.0E-5 or even 0.00001. And to say what is meant without bombast, all three lines should be changed to

```
IF (ABS(B-A) .LT. 1.0E-5) GOTO 3
```

The test now reads clearly; it is merely wrong.

If X is large, it is quite possible that the absolute difference between successive trial roots will never be less than the arbitrary threshold of 1.0E-5 unless it is exactly zero, because of the finite precision with which computers represent numbers. It is a delicate question of numerical analysis whether this difference will always become zero. For small values of X, on the other hand, the criterion will be met long before a good approximation is attained. But if we replace the absolute convergence criterion by a test of whether the estimate is close enough *relative to the original data,* we should get five place accuracy for most positive arguments:

```
C COMPUTE SQUARE ROOTS BY NEWTON'S METHOD
 100   READ(5,110) X
 110      FORMAT(F10.0)
C
       IF (X .LT. 0.0) WRITE(6,120) X
 120      FORMAT(1X, 'SQRT(', 1PE12.4, ') UNDEFINED')
C
       IF (X .EQ. 0.0) WRITE(6,130) X, X
 130      FORMAT(1X, 'SQRT(', 1PE12.4, ') = ', 1PE12.4)
C
       IF (X .LE. 0.0) GOTO 100
       B = X/2.0
 200   IF (ABS(X/B - B) .LT. 1.0E-5 * B) GOTO 300
       B = (X/B + B) / 2.0
       GOTO 200
 300   WRITE(6,130) X, B
       GOTO 100
       END
```

The modified program is still not a typical square root routine, nor do we wish to go into the detailed treatment of floating point arithmetic needed to make it one. The original example is, however, typical of programs in general: it profits from criticism and revision.

Let us conclude the chapter with another example that illustrates several failings. This program is a sorting routine.

```
      DIMENSION N(500)
      WRITE (6,6)
    6 FORMAT (1H1,26HNUMBERS IN ALGEBRAIC ORDER)
      DO 8 I=1,500
    8 READ (5,7) N(I)
    7 FORMAT (I4)
      DO 10 K=1,1999
      J=K-1000
      DO 10 I-1,500
      IF(N(I)-J)10,9,10
   10 CONTINUE
      STOP
    9 WRITE (6,95) N(I)
   95 FORMAT (1H ,I4)
      GO TO 10
      END
```

The code suffers not only from lack of generality, but from an ill-advised algorithm, some dubious coding practices, and even a typographical error. The line

```
      DO 10 I-1,500
```

is wrong: the "−" should be "=". The program was contrived in part to illustrate that the range of a DO loop can be extended by a transfer outside and back, even though in this case the inner DO loop *and* the code of the extended range can all be better written in line as

```
      DO 10 I = 1, 500
         IF (N(I) .EQ. J) WRITE (6,95) N(I)
   95       FORMAT(1X, I4)
   10 CONTINUE
```

More to the point is the question of whether programmers should be encouraged to use extended ranges in the first place. Jumping around unnecessarily in a computer program has proved to be a fruitful source of errors, and usually indicates that the programmer is not entirely in control of the code. The apparently random statement numbers in this example are often a symptom of the same disorder.

The program has other flaws. It reads in 500 numbers, one per card, and sorts them about as inefficiently as possible — by comparing each number with all integers between −999 and +999. It does this once, for only one set of numbers, then stops.

But wait. With an I4 input format, it is possible to read positive numbers as large as 9999, since we can leave out the plus sign; the program as it stands will fail to list four-digit numbers. To correct the oversight will slow the algorithm by a factor of more than five, without extending its generality in the least. Extending this method to handle larger integers would slow it by orders of magnitude, and to ask it to handle floating point numbers would be unthinkable.

We will not attempt to rewrite this code, since we disagree with its basic approach. (Chapter 7 contains several better sorting programs.) We just want to show that the same program can be viewed from different perspectives, and that the job of critical reading doesn't end when you find a typo or even a poor coding practice. In the chapters to come we will explore the issues touched on here and several others that strongly affect programming style.

We begin, in Chapter 2, with a study of how to express individual statements clearly. Writing arithmetic expressions and conditional (IF) statements is usually the first aspect of computer programming that is taught. It is important to master these fundamentals before becoming too involved with other language features.

Chapter 3 treats the control-flow structure of computer programs, that is, how flow of control is specified through looping and decision-making statements. It also shows how data can be represented to make programming as easy as possible, and how data structure can be used to derive a clean control flow. Program structure is covered in Chapter 4, how to break up a program into manageable pieces. Considerable emphasis is given in these chapters to proper use of structured programming and sound design techniques.

Chapter 5 examines input and output: how to render programs less vulnerable to bad input data and what to output to obtain maximum benefit from a run. A number of common blunders are studied in Chapter 6, and tips are given on how to spot such errors and correct them.

Contrary to popular practice, efficiency and documentation are reserved for the last two chapters, 7 and 8. While both of these topics are important and warrant study, we feel they have received proportionately too much attention — particularly in introductory courses — at the expense of clarity and general good style.

A few words on the ground rules we have used in criticizing programs:

(1) Programs are presented in a form as close to the original as our typescript permits. Formatting, typographical errors, and syntax errors are as in the original. (Exception: three PL/I programs have been translated from the 48-character set into the 60-character set.)

(2) We regularly abstract parts of programs to focus better on the essential points. We believe that the failings we discuss are inherent in the code shown, and not caused or aggravated by abstracting. We have tried not to quote out of context. We have tried throughout to solve essentially the same problem as the original version did, so comparisons may be made fairly, even though this sometimes means that we do not make all possible improvements in programs.

(3) We will not fault an example for using non-standard language features (for example, mixed mode arithmetic in Fortran) unless the use is quite unusual or dangerous. Most compilers accept non-standard constructions, and standards themselves change with time. Remember, though, that unusual features are rarely portable, and are the least resistant to changes in their environment.

Our own Fortran hews closely to the 1966 American National Standards Institute (ANSI) version, except for our use of quoted Hollerith strings (we refuse to count characters). PL/I programs meet the standard set by IBM's checkout compiler, version 1, release 3.0. Although there are new versions of Fortran and PL/I in sight which will make better programming possible in both of these languages, they are not yet widespread, so we have not written any examples in the newer dialects.

(4) In our discussions of numerical algorithms (like the square root routine above) we will not try to treat all possible pathological cases; the defenses needed against overflow, significance loss, and other numerical pitfalls are beyond the scope of this book. But we do insist that at least the rudimentary precautions be taken, like using relative tests instead of absolute and avoiding division by zero, to ensure good results for reasonable inputs.

(5) Every line of code in this book has been compiled, directly from the text, which is in machine-readable form. All of our programs have been tested (Fortran on a Honeywell 6070, PL/I on an IBM 370/168). Our Fortran programs have also been run through a verifier to monitor compliance with the ANSI standard.

Nevertheless, mistakes can occur. We encourage you to view with suspicion anything we say that looks peculiar. Test it, try it out. Don't treat computer output as gospel. If you learn to be wary of everyone else's programs, you will be better able to check your own.

POINTS TO PONDER

1.1   A matrix with n rows and n columns has n^2 elements. So to initialize such a matrix requires n^2 assignments. To multiply two n by n matrices together, or to solve n linear equations in n unknowns, involves on the order of n^3 operations by classical methods. (These are the sorts of things that matrix manipulation programs do.) Give arguments to support the following conjectures:

If $n \geqslant 10$, the time required to initialize a matrix is not very important.

If $n < 10$, the time required to initialize a matrix is not very important. (Hint: input and output conversions are more time consuming than arithmetic.)

1.2   In the first edition of this book, we wrote the square root routine this way:

```
C               COMPUTE SQUARE ROOTS BY NEWTON'S METHOD
    10 READ(5,11) X
    11 FORMAT (F10.0)
       IF (X .GE. 0.0) GOTO 20
          WRITE(6,13) X
    13    FORMAT (' SQRT(', 1PE12.5, ') UNDEFINED')
          GOTO 10
    20 IF (X .GT. 0.0) GOTO 30
          B = 0.0
          GOTO 50
    30 B = 1.0
    40    A = B
          B = (X/A + A)/2.0
          IF (ABS((X/B)/B - 1.0) .GE. 1.0E-5) GOTO 40
    50 WRITE(6,51) X, B
    51 FORMAT(' SQRT(', 1PE12.5, ') = ', 1PE12.5)
          GOTO 10
          END
```

This is "more efficient" because there are no repeated tests. Which version do you prefer, and why? How much time and space difference does the change make? What deficiencies of the Fortran language are illustrated by both versions?

1.3   In the square root routine, we saw that testing for convergence against an absolute threshold like 1.0E-5 is perilous. We recommended testing instead against some sort of relative standard. How can the function

```
          REAL FUNCTION RELDIF(X, Y)
          RELDIF = ABS(X - Y) / AMAX1(ABS(X), ABS(Y))
          RETURN
          END
```

be used in the example? (AMAX1 is the Fortran function that returns the maximum of two or more floating point numbers as floating point.) This function is relatively well-behaved for values that might be encountered in the square-root routine. In more general applications, are there any values of X and Y that might cause trouble?

Writing a computer program eventually boils down to writing a sequence of statements in the language at hand. How each of those statements is expressed determines in large measure the intelligibility of the whole; no amount of commenting, formatting, or supplementary documentation can entirely replace well expressed statements. After all, they determine what the program actually *does*.

It is easy to mistake a sequence of overly-simple expressions for profundity. An extreme example of this is

```
    IF(X .LT. Y) GO TO 30
    IF (Y .LT. Z) GO TO 50
    SMALL = Z
    GO TO 70
 30 IF (X .LT. Z) GO TO 60
    SMALL = Z
    GO TO 70
 50 SMALL = Y
    GO TO 70
 60 SMALL = X
 70 ...
```

Ten lines, with four statement numbers and six GOTO's; surely *something* is happening. Before reading further, test yourself. What does this program do?

The mnemonic SMALL is a giveaway — the sequence sets SMALL to the smallest of X, Y, and Z.

There are a number of ways to do this computation. If our purpose is to teach how to compute the minimum, we write

```
    SMALL = X
    IF (Y .LT. SMALL) SMALL = Y
    IF (Z .LT. SMALL) SMALL = Z
```

which is direct and to the point. Labels and GOTO's are not needed. And the generalization to computing the minimum of many elements is obvious.

Say what you mean, simply and directly.

But if we are just trying to get the job done, we use the Fortran built-in function AMIN1, which computes the minimum of two or more floating point numbers:

9

```
SMALL = AMIN1(X, Y, Z)
```

One line replaces ten. How can a piece of code that is an order of magnitude too large be considered reliable? There is that much greater chance for confusion, and hence for the introduction of bugs. There is that much more that must be understood in order to make changes.

Library functions like AMIN1 are one way to reduce the apparent complexity of a program; they help to keep program size manageable, and they let you build on the work of others, instead of starting from scratch each time.

Use library functions.

Code that is excessively clever is at least as hard to understand as code that is too simple-minded. For example,

```
DCL TEXT CHAR(200)VAR;
GET LIST(TEXT);
N=0;
START: A=INDEX(TEXT,' ');
IF A=0 THEN GO TO FINISH;
N=N+1;
TEXT=SUBSTR(TEXT,A+1);
GO TO START;
FINISH: PUT LIST(N);
```

Even though this uses PL/I's built-in functions INDEX and SUBSTR, it is hardly clear. INDEX(TEXT,' ') returns the position of the first blank in TEXT, or zero if there is no blank. SUBSTR(TEXT,A+1) produces the substring of TEXT that begins at position A+1; this is re-assigned to TEXT, thus disposing of characters up to and including the leftmost remaining blank. So after a bit of thought, we can see that this program counts the number of blanks in TEXT.

Suppose that you were trying to teach a novice programmer how to count the blanks in a character string? How would you do it? Surely not by this elegant but mystifying method — instead you would say "Look at each character, and if it's a blank, count it." Or, in PL/I,

```
DECLARE TEXT CHARACTER(200) VARYING;
GET LIST (TEXT);
N = 0;
DO I = 1 TO LENGTH(TEXT);
   IF SUBSTR(TEXT, I, 1) = ' ' THEN
        N = N + 1;
END;
PUT LIST (N);
```

This too uses the built-in functions that PL/I provides, but it uses them in a way that clarifies the method of solution, rather than obscuring it. Everyone knows that debugging is twice as hard as writing a program in the first place. So if you're as clever as you can be when you write it, how will you ever debug it?

Peculiar modes of expression often arise out of attempts to write "efficient" code. The programmer has some knowledge about how a particular compiler generates code, and so uses only those expressions "known" to be "better." For instance

```
10  F1=X1-X2*X2
    F2=1.0-X2
    FX=F1*F1+F2*F2
C NOTE THAT IT IS MORE EFFICIENT TO COMPUTE
C F1*F1 THAN TO COMPUTE F1**2.
```

Whether "efficient" means "takes less time" or "takes fewer machine instructions," the comment is not always true. Many compilers recognize the special case F1**2 and generate the same code as for F1*F1. Some compilers would, in fact, generate shorter and faster code for

```
10  FX = (X1 - X2**2)**2 + (1.0 - X2)**2
```

than for the original version. (Ours produced 15 instructions for the original version, 13 for the revision.)

This rendition also happens to be more readable and eliminates the temporary variables F1 and F2, which have little mnemonic value. The fewer temporary variables in a program, the less chance there is that one will not be properly initialized, or that one will be altered unexpectedly before it is used. "Temporary" is a dirty word in programming — it suggests that a variable can be used with less thought than a "normal" (permanent?) one, and it encourages the use of one variable for several unrelated calculations. Both are dangerous practices.

Avoid temporary variables.

Even if the comment about efficiency were true in a particular environment, there is still little justification for using the more obscure mode of expression. We shall discuss the question of efficiency further in Chapter 7. For now, we observe simply that a program usually has to be read several times in the process of getting it debugged. The harder it is for *people* to grasp the intent of any given section, the longer it will be before the program becomes operational. Trying to outsmart a compiler defeats much of the purpose of using one.

Write clearly — don't sacrifice clarity for "efficiency."

A variation of this is

```
/*   NOTE THAT '110010' IN BINARY IS '50' IN DECIMAL   */
/*         THIS WILL BE USED FOR LINE COUNTING          */
    ...
          IF NO>101111B THEN DO ; PUT PAGE; NO=0B;
                END;
```

The programmer evidently hopes to avoid a run-time type-conversion by using FIXED BINARY constants in expressions involving FIXED BINARY variables. The comment underlines the fact that human beings are not likely to know the binary representation of 50. Yet we are expected to recognize a binary 47 on the basis of this one hint. One of the first services to be automated in early computer languages was the conversion of decimal to binary. It would be a shame if we were forced to think in binary, after all these years, by misinformed considerations of "efficiency." (Most compilers will convert "47" to binary at compile time, by the way. Those that will not must certainly provide worse inefficiencies to worry about.)

The proper thing to do here is to introduce a parameter, such as MAXLINES, and initialize it to 47 once and for all at the top of the program. The code becomes much more readable and easier to change. And if there happens to be an expensive conversion, it will occur only once.

Let the machine do the dirty work.

Repeated patterns of code catch the eye when scanning listings. Since the computer is a tool for handling repetitious operations, we should be alerted by such patterns to look for oversights — why didn't the programmer let the computer do the repeating? In the middle of a program for manipulating triangles we see the fragment

```
C       COMPUTE LENGTHS OF SIDES
        AB = SQRT((X2 - X1)**2 + (Y2 - Y1)**2)
        AC = SQRT((X3 - X1)**2 + (Y3 - Y1)**2)
        BC = SQRT((X3 - X2)**2 + (Y3 - Y2)**2)
C       COMPUTE AREA
        S = (AB + BC + AC) / 2.0
        AREA = SQRT(S * (S-BC) * (S-AC) * (S-AB))
        ...
C       COMPUTE ANGLES
        ALPHA = ATANF((4.0*AREA) / (AC**2 + AB**2 - BC**2))
        BETA  = ATANF((4.0*AREA) / (AB**2 + BC**2 - AC**2))
        GAMMA = ATANF((4.0*AREA) / (AC**2 + BC**2 - AB**2))
```

We can see immediately the advantage of defining two arithmetic statement functions:

```
        SIDE(XA, YA, XB, YB) = SQRT((XA-XB)**2 + (YA-YB)**2)
        ANGLE(SAREA, SA, SB, SC) = ATAN2(4.0*SAREA, SA**2 + SB**2 - SC**2)
```

so that we can write

```
        AB = SIDE(X1, Y1, X2, Y2)
        AC = SIDE(X1, Y1, X3, Y3)
        BC = SIDE(X2, Y2, X3, Y3)
        ...
        ALPHA = ANGLE(AREA, AC, AB, BC)
        BETA  = ANGLE(AREA, AB, BC, AC)
        GAMMA = ANGLE(AREA, AC, BC, AB)
```

This is not only easier to write but also easier to modify. For instance the Fortran II name ATANF should be changed whenever possible to the Fortran IV standard ATAN. In fact, the form

```
        ATAN(Y/X)
```

should always be changed to

```
        ATAN2(Y, X)
```

which correctly handles right-angled triangles instead of causing a division by zero
when Y/X is evaluated. Only one change was needed in the function definition to
correct all three calculations; we were more likely to get it right. (The program also
contains a typographical error:

```
        AREA = SQRT(S * (S-BC) * (S-AC) * (S-AB)
```

needs a balancing right parenthesis on the end.)

Fortran's arithmetic statement function is unfortunately restricted to one-line
expressions, and is thus of limited usefulness. When the operation to be done is
more complex, write a separate subroutine or function. The ease of later
comprehending, debugging, and changing the program will more than compensate
for any overhead caused by adding the extra modules.

Replace repetitive expressions by calls
to a common function.

Another eye-catching repeat appears in

```
        R = 12.
        AL = 24.
        TIME = 0.
        THETA = 0.
        DELTH = 2. * 3.1416 / 100.
        DO 18 I = 1,100
        X = R*(1. - COS(THETA)) + L - L*SQRT(1. - (R*SIN(THETA)/L)**2)
        THETA = THETA + DELTH
        XNEW= R * (1. - COS(THETA)) + L - L*SQRT(1. - (R*SIN(THETA)/L)**2)
        VEL = (XNEW - X) / 0.01
        TIME = TIME + 0.01
     18 WRITE (2,8) TIME, THETA, XNEW, VEL
      8 FORMAT (4F9.2)
        STOP
        END
```

Our first impulse is to define another arithmetic statement function for the gangling
expression that appears twice, but closer inspection shows a more fundamental oversight.

The program computes X and its first derivative VEL at each of 100 successive
points. Two adjacent values of X must be known to find VEL, so the program duti-
fully computes both on each iteration, even though one value is already known from
the previous iteration. The elaborate expression is computed twice as often as
necessary. Worse, it is written twice, which increases the risk that one occurrence
will be modified and the other overlooked.

There is also an error: L is used in both expressions where AL is certainly
intended. Less serious, but potentially troublesome, is the practice of incrementing
a floating point variable many times (see Chapter 6). To keep arithmetic errors

from piling up and to make the code clearer, we are better off computing `TIME` and `THETA` from `I` on each iteration. Putting everything together gives:

```
       REAL L
       R = 12.0
       L = 24.0
       X = 0.0
       DO 20 I = 1, 100
           TIME = FLOAT(I)/100.0
           THETA = 2.0 * 3.141593 * TIME
           XNEW = R * (1.0 - COS(THETA)) + L -
     $             L * SQRT(1.0 - (R*SIN(THETA)/L)**2)
           VEL = (XNEW - X)/0.01
           WRITE(2,10) TIME, THETA, XNEW, VEL
    10     FORMAT(4F9.2)
           X = XNEW
    20 CONTINUE
       STOP
       END
```

(We have used $ as the continuation character, because it is the only standard Fortran character without any other syntactic meaning. It minimizes the chance for confusion, and is likely to cause a visible error if used in the wrong column.)

Since we have saved a hundred function evaluations, we will not worry about computing 2π inside the loop. We also decided to stick with the identifier `L`, instead of changing all occurrences to `AL`. The original problem was stated in terms of `R` and `L`; it is usually safer to remain consistent with this notation than to try to remember the translation all the time. This is one of those unfortunate occasions when standard Fortran notation is at odds with the usage desired. You can argue it either way, but we decided in this case that adding the statement

```
       REAL L
```

is better than renaming the variable. If you get into the habit of declaring *all* variables, the problem doesn't arise at all.

Arithmetic expressions in Fortran and PL/I also differ sometimes from the way we intuitively tend to write them. We are accustomed, in writing algebra, to bind multiplication tighter than division. That is, we assume that if we write

```
       A*B/2.0*C
```

it means

```
       (A*B)/(2.0*C)   /* WRONG */
```

But in Fortran and PL/I the interpretation is

```
       ((A*B)/2.0)*C
```

Only by using parentheses or rearranging the computation can we avoid potential confusion.

A more insidious operator ambiguity occurs in this expression from an arctangent routine:

```
       TERM = TERM*(-X**2)/DENOM
```

Is X negated and then squared, or is it squared and then negated? Fortran reference manuals seldom treat such fine points in detail; this may be a hard question to answer without running a test program. As a matter of fact the ANSI standard for Fortran calls for the latter interpretation (fortunate in this case) — the variable X is squared and then negated — but the line should still be rewritten as:

```
TERM = -TERM * X**2 / DENOM
```

The first form invites misunderstanding on the part of the reader, if not the compiler. Unless reader and compiler both understand the writer, the program is not communicating properly.

Parenthesize to avoid ambiguity.

Variable names can also be either safe or dangerous:

```
8 NO5S = NO5S + 1
```

Now was that "N, letter O, five, S," or "N, zero, five, S," or even "NOSS"? The possibilities for error are numerous. Would you trust someone else to type corrections for this program? Mixtures of similar characters (letter O and digit 0, letter I and digit 1, etc.) are unsafe, as are long identifiers that differ only at the end. Use XPOS and YPOS, not POSITIONX and POSITIONY. When abbreviating, always keep first letters, favor "pronounceable" forms (XPOS, not XPSTN), and above all be consistent.

Similar identifiers are dangerous in general. One program contains the improbable sequence

```
N = K
N = K**2
NNN = K**3
```

It is only when, much further down, we read

```
WRITE(6,60)N,NN,NNN, ...
```

that the typographical error in the second line becomes clear. A better choice of names here is N, NSQ, NCUBE. Try to choose names that differ widely; typos and misspellings are less likely to be disguised. Of course, choose names that mean something as well, so the intent of the code is clearer. (We will discuss this more in Chapter 8.)

Choose variable names that won't be confused.

We have discussed arithmetic expressions quite a bit, but conditional expressions are at least as important in writing programs. In either PL/I or Fortran, conditional expressions nearly always involve at least one IF statement, which controls whether or not another statement is executed, on the basis of some condition. PL/I allows the controlled statement to be compound, and therefore arbitrarily complex, but we will save more complicated examples for Chapter 3. Some of the worst examples of misused conditional expressions are in Fortran, since the limited facilities of that language encourage greater atrocities.

Part of the reason for this is historical. Fortran II had only the arithmetic IF statement, which does not perform as we suggested in the previous paragraph. Instead it causes a branch to one of three statement numbers, depending on whether an arithmetic expression is negative, zero, or positive. The logical IF was added to Fortran IV as a cleaner way of expressing conditionals. It should always be used instead of the arithmetic IF, especially since two of the three labels are almost always the same in practice.

One of the most productive ways to make a program easier to understand is to reduce the degree of interdependence between statements, so that each part can be studied and understood in relative isolation. One of the major liabilities of the Fortran arithmetic IF is that it *increases* the connections between statements:

```
50 IF(C-COMMA) 55,70,55
55 IF(C-SCOL)  60,70,60
60 IF(C-DASH)  65,70,65
65 NC=NC+1
70 ...
```

The wall-to-wall statement numbers are the first thing to strike the eye. The first line says that if C-COMMA is negative or positive, control transfers to statement 55; if it is zero, control goes to 70. In other words, if C equals COMMA, branch to 70; if not, fall through to the next statement, 55. Similar reasoning applies at statements 55 and 60.

Putting everything together, if C is not a comma and C is not a semicolon and C is not a dash, the statement NC=NC+1 is executed. Or, in Fortran,

```
50 IF (C.NE.COMMA .AND. C.NE.SCOL .AND. C.NE.DASH) NC = NC + 1
```

Most people "understand" an arithmetic IF by mentally translating it into a logical IF, just as we did here. There is little reason ever to use an arithmetic IF.

There is another difficulty with the arithmetic IF version of this program. All those labels in the left margin represent potential targets for branches from other parts of the program. Without reading through *all* of the program from which this excerpt comes, you can't be certain that no other statement branches into the middle of the construction. But when the group of statements is collapsed into a single IF, there is no doubt about how to get to it — it is entered at the beginning and exited at the end, and it has no other connections with the rest of the program. The logical IF reduces the apparent complexity of the program.

Occasionally the third branch of an arithmetic IF can serve to direct an "impossible" condition to error-handling code. It is always good practice to think through such conditions and deal with them properly. Even when all three branches of the arithmetic IF are distinct, however, readability is better served by substituting two logical IF's and a GOTO.

Avoid the Fortran arithmetic IF.

The influence of the arithmetic IF often extends into misuse of the logical IF. For example,

```
IF((X(I) - X(N)) .LE. 0.) GO TO 300
```

is a literal translation of an arithmetic into a logical IF, which should be written

```
IF (X(I) .LE. X(N)) GOTO 300
```

("Say what you mean.") And

```
IF (MOD(K,N1).NE.0) GO TO 9
WRITE (6,4) K,X
9 ...
```

is better rendered as

```
IF (MOD(K,N1) .EQ. 0) WRITE (6,4) K, X
```

The same observation holds for PL/I:

```
GROSSPAY = BASERATE *
   TOTALHRS;
IF TOTALHRS <= 40 THEN GO TO
   NOVT;
GROSSPAY = GROSSPAY + 0.5 *
   BASERATE * (TOTALHRS - 40);
NOVT: ...
```

Since the GOTO branches around only a single statement, it is clearly unnecessary. Rewriting gives

```
GROSSPAY = BASERATE * TOTALHRS;
IF TOTALHRS > 40 THEN
   GROSSPAY = GROSSPAY + 0.5 * BASERATE * (TOTALHRS-40);
```

A conditional expression can also be disguised by using a Fortran computed GOTO:

```
GOTO(65,70),PRNT
65 WRITE(6,105) X
70 ...
```

The computed GOTO has a definite place, but this is not it. Since labels 65 and 70 appear nowhere else in the program, this code is certainly better written as

```
IF (PRNT .NE. 2) WRITE (6,105) X
```

to eliminate the two statement numbers. Now we can tell at a glance that there is only one way to reach the WRITE statement.

These last three examples show a tendency to follow all IF's with branches, even when they do not have to be. Such usage eventually leads to circumlocutions like

```
      GRVAL = A(1)
      DO 25 I = 2,10
      IF (A(I).GT.GRVAL) GO TO 30
      GO TO 25
   30 GRVAL = A(I)
   25 CONTINUE
```

The IF controls a branch that branches around the branch that branches around the statement we wanted to do in the first place! Turning things right side up gives

```
      GRVAL = A(1)
      DO 25 I = 2,10
          IF (A(I) .GT. GRVAL) GRVAL = A(I)
   25 CONTINUE
```

We leave it to the reader to decide whether the IF statement should be replaced by

```
      GRVAL = AMAX1(GRVAL, A(I))
```

when we are finding the larger of just two elements.

Avoid unnecessary branches.

Even though PL/I has adequate facilities for writing programs without any branches at all, they are often neglected, in a style of coding called "Fortran with semicolons." Abuse of PL/I ultimately leads to code like this sorting routine:

```
      DO  M = 1 TO N;
      K =  N-1;
      DO J = 1 TO K;
      IF ARAY(J) - ARAY(J+1) >= 0
                  THEN GO TO RETRN;
                       ELSE;
      SAVE = ARAY(J);
      ARAY(J) = ARAY(J+1);
      ARAY(J+1) = SAVE;
RETRN:    END;
      END;
```

The construction THEN GOTO might be an early exit from a loop, but more often is a tipoff that something is amiss. Here it only branches around three statements, not out of the loop. Why not turn the test around so no GOTO or label is required? (The ELSE with no statement after it, a "null ELSE," serves no purpose whatsoever; it only confuses the issue.) Subtraction and comparison against zero is a bad idea because of the danger of overflow or underflow; a direct comparison would be safer and far easier to understand. The outer loop need only be done N-1 times, and the inner N-M times. Of course PL/I allows expressions in the limits of DO loops, so there is no need for the temporary variable K. And the erratic indentation should be changed so it tells how the statements are related to each other. Putting these improvements all together gives

```
        DO M = 1 TO N-1;
          DO J = 1 TO N-M;
            IF ARAY(J) < ARAY(J+1) THEN DO;
              SAVE = ARAY(J);
              ARAY(J) = ARAY(J+1);
              ARAY(J+1) = SAVE;
            END;
          END;
        END;
```

---

*Use the good features of a language;
avoid the bad ones.*

A failure to state clearly the underlying logic can lead to tangled control flow, as in this program for a rudimentary computer dating service:

```
      LOGICAL FEM(8),MALE(8)
      READ(5,6)IGIRL,(FEM(I),I=1,8)
    9 READ(5,6)IBOY,(MALE(I),I=1,8)
      DO 8I= 1,8
      IF(FEM(I)) GO TO 7
      IF(.NOT.MALE(I)) GO TO 8
      GO TO 9
    7 IF(.NOT.MALE(I)) GO TO 9
    8 CONTINUE
      WRITE(2,10) IBOY
    6 FORMAT (I5,8L1)
   10 FORMAT (10X,I5)
      GO TO 9
      STOP
      END
```

We have to look long and hard at this jungle of IF's and GOTO's before the light dawns. The program is supposed to write IBOY only if each of the MALE(I) has the same truth value as the corresponding FEM(I). Standard Fortran does not allow us to ask directly if two LOGICAL variables are equal or not, but we can still improve readability by using .AND. and .OR.:

```
      LOGICAL FEM(8), MALE(8)
      READ (5,10) IGIRL, FEM
   10    FORMAT (I5, 8L1)
   20 READ (5,10) IBOY, MALE
      DO 30 I = 1, 8
        IF ((FEM(I) .AND. .NOT.MALE(I)) .OR.
      $     (MALE(I) .AND. .NOT.FEM(I))) GOTO 20
   30 CONTINUE
      WRITE (2,40) IBOY
   40    FORMAT (10X, I5)
      GOTO 20
      END
```

This tells us directly that the program will go on to read the next input line, without printing IBOY, if any one of the FEM(I) differs from its corresponding MALE(I).

We also deleted the inaccessible STOP statement and the explicit indexing in the READ statements, indented the code, and numbered the statements systematically.

Don't use conditional branches as a substitute for a logical expression.

As an aside, the dating program provides a simple example of how an appropriate data representation can make programming easier. With INTEGER variables instead of LOGICAL, we can make the desired comparison directly:

```
         INTEGER FEM(8), MALE(8)
         READ (5,10) IGIRL, FEM
   10    FORMAT (I5, 8I1)
   20 READ (5,10) IBOY, MALE
         DO 30 I = 1, 8
            IF (FEM(I) .NE. MALE(I)) GOTO 20
   30 CONTINUE
         ...
```

The data will also have to be changed, from T's and F's to ones and zeros, but this is a simple mechanical operation. We will discuss data structure at more length in Chapter 3.

The expression in parentheses in a logical IF statement is of type LOGICAL; its value is either .TRUE. or .FALSE.. Most of the time we use just a relational operator, such as .LE. or .EQ., to determine the truth value of the condition. But we can, if we wish, use the Boolean operators .AND., .OR., and .NOT. to make arbitrarily complex logical expressions. Boolean algebra is not used nearly as widely as ordinary arithmetic, so we must write logical expressions more carefully lest we confuse the reader.

Consider the sequence

```
   6 IF(X1.GE.ARRAY(I)) GO TO 2
      IF(ARRAY(I).LT.X2) ICOUNT=ICOUNT+1
   2 ...
```

It takes a while to realize that ICOUNT is incremented only if ARRAY(I) lies between X1 and X2. Inversions and GOTO's slow down reading comprehension and should be avoided. Rewriting gives:

```
   6 IF (ARRAY(I).GT.X1 .AND. ARRAY(I).LT.X2) ICOUNT = ICOUNT + 1
```

It is much easier to tell at a glance what the logic implies.

Logical conditions can often be combined *if* they are all related, and if they are combined with only a single type of operator. For example,

```
      IF(NUM.LT.0000000)GO TO 500
      IF(NUM.GT.9999999)GO TO 500
      IF(AMON.LT.00000000)GO TO 500
      IF(AMON.GT.99999999)GO TO 500
      IF(ITEM.LT.0000)GO TO 500
      IF(ITEM.GT.9999)GO TO 500
      GO TO 150
  500 WRITE(6,80)NUM,CUST,AMON,ITEM,IMM,IDD,IYY
      GO TO 150
```

Leaving aside the redundant zeros (after all, zero is zero, so adding more digits won't make it more precise), there is a suspicious regularity to the code: everything heads for statement 500.

Combining the logical conditions gives us the following version:

```
      IF (NUM .LT. 0 .OR. NUM .GT. 9999999
  $      .OR. AMON .LT. 0 .OR. AMON .GT. 99999999
  $      .OR. ITEM .LT. 0 .OR. ITEM .GT. 9999)
  $         WRITE(6,80) NUM, CUST, AMON, ITEM, IMM, IDD, IYY
      GO TO 150
```

This is still quite a mouthful, but since each part of the test has the same structure, and the parts are all combined with the same operator, it can be readily understood.

It is simpler to write good logical expressions in PL/I, but that is no guarantee that all expressions will be written as clearly as they can be:

```
      IF K=0 | (¬(PRINT='YES' | PRINT='NO')) THEN DO;
```

The inversion and double parentheses slow comprehension. It seems better to distribute the "not" operation through the parenthesized expression. De Morgan's rules

```
      ¬(A | B)   <=>   ¬A & ¬B
      ¬(A & B)   <=>   ¬A | ¬B
```

tell us how:

```
      IF K = 0 | (PRINT ¬= 'YES' & PRINT ¬= 'NO') THEN DO;
```

The expression is still not simple, but it is now in a form that more closely resembles how we speak. Note that we elected to keep the parentheses, even though none are necessary here, to make the operator binding unambiguous to the reader as well as the compiler.

A useful way to decide if some piece of code is clear or not is the "telephone test." If someone could understand your code when read aloud over the telephone, it's clear enough. If not, then it needs rewriting.

Use the "telephone test" for readability.

Judicious use of De Morgan's rules often improves the readability of programs by simplifying logical expressions. But care should be exercised in how they are applied. An example of the pitfalls of inverting logic comes from this routine to access a sparse matrix stored as a linear table. The function is supposed to return a table value if it finds a matching row *and* column; otherwise it returns zero.

```
      FUNCTION SPARSE(I,J)
      COMMON /SP/ N,NROW(500),NCOL(500),VALUE(500)
      DO 10 K = 1,N
      IF (NROW(K).NE.I .AND. NCOL(K).NE.J) GO TO 10
      SPARSE = VALUE(K)
      GO TO 999
   10 CONTINUE
      SPARSE = 0.0
  999 RETURN
      END
```

By definition the sparse array has a value stored at VALUE(K) for (I,J) if

```
      NROW(K).EQ.I .AND. NCOL(K).EQ.J
```

Negating this for the IF statement gives

```
      .NOT.(NROW(K).EQ.I) .OR. .NOT.(NCOL(K).EQ.J)
```

which in turn is

```
      NROW(K).NE.I .OR. NCOL(K).NE.J
```

Compare this line with the IF statement in the function. The function SPARSE is wrong; it will return the first value where *either* I or J is matched. The .AND. must be changed to .OR.. (This error has been corrected in later printings of the text from which it was taken.) Actually, the code would be more direct if it were written with the test stated the way a human reader would say it:

```
      FUNCTION SPARSE(I, J)
      COMMON /SP/ N, NROW(500), NCOL(500), VALUE(500)
      DO 10 K = 1,N
          IF (NROW(K).EQ.I .AND. NCOL(K).EQ.J) GOTO 20
   10 CONTINUE
      SPARSE = 0.0
      RETURN
C
   20 SPARSE = VALUE(K)
      RETURN
      END
```

We have discussed a number of small examples where expressions were either hard to read, misleading, or downright incorrect. Let us conclude this chapter with a larger example, to show how quickly a program can get out of hand when you fail to look after the little things. (This is the first big PL/I program we have looked at — don't let it frighten you.) The program finds the area under the parabola $y=x^2$ between $x=0$ and $x=1$, using a trapezoidal rule, for several different step sizes.

```
TRAPZ: PROCEDURE OPTIONS (MAIN);
       DECLARE MSSG1 CHARACTER (20);
         MSSG1 = 'AREA UNDER THE CURVE';
       DECLARE MSSG2 CHARACTER (23);
         MSSG2 = 'BY THE TRAPAZOIDAL RULE';
       DECLARE MSSG3 CHARACTER (16);
         MSSG3 = 'FOR DELTA X = 1/';
       DECLARE I FIXED DECIMAL (2);
       DECLARE J FIXED DECIMAL (2);
       DECLARE L FIXED DECIMAL (7,6);
       DECLARE M FIXED DECIMAL (7,6);
       DECLARE N FIXED DECIMAL (2);
       DECLARE AREA1 FIXED DECIMAL (8,6);
       DECLARE AREA FIXED DECIMAL  (8,6);
       DECLARE LMTS FIXED DECIMAL (5,4);
          PUT SKIP EDIT (MSSG1)  (X(9), A(20));
          PUT SKIP EDIT (MSSG2) (X(7), A(23));
          PUT SKIP EDIT (' ') (A(1));
        AREA = 0;
             DO K = 4 TO 10;
               M = 1 / K;
               N = K - 1;
        LMTS = .5 * M;
           I = 1;
             DO J = 1 TO N;
               L = (I / K) ** 2;
        AREA1 = .5 * M * (2 * L);
        AREA = AREA + AREA1;
           IF I = N THEN CALL OUT;
             ELSE I = I + 1;
        END;
      END;
  OUT: PROCEDURE;
       AREA = AREA + LMTS;
      PUT SKIP EDIT  (MSSG3,K,AREA) (X(2),A(16),F(2),X(6),
           F(9,6));
       AREA = 0;
      RETURN;
    END;
  END;
```

Held at arm's length, this program looks pretty impressive. There is a large assortment of data declarations, followed by a computation that is evidently complex enough to warrant a sub-procedure. Declarations are neatly aligned, and the executable statements are staggered so as to indicate several levels of control nesting. There are text strings to suggest the intent of the program, and mnemonic identifiers to give hints about how the results are obtained. The general impression conveyed is that this is a moderately complicated problem that has been carefully coded and is now well under control.

Closer inspection, however, shows quite the opposite.

Each output message is used only once, and would be better placed in the PUT statement that uses it instead of being separately declared and initialized by an assignment. (One message is even misspelled.) The first two PUT statements can be combined into

```
PUT SKIP EDIT ('AREA UNDER THE CURVE',
               'BY THE TRAPEZOIDAL RULE')
              (X(9), A, SKIP, X(7), A);
```

and the bizarre

```
PUT SKIP EDIT(' ') (A(1));
```

changed into a simple `PUT SKIP`. And there is no reason to specify character-string lengths in the A format items; computers count much better than people do.

The purpose of the assignment

```
M = 1 / K;
```

is unclear. Does it defend against some mysterious conversion? Is it to convey geometrical insight? Or does the programmer worry that computers divide more slowly than they multiply? It is a rare program that can be speeded up significantly by changing divisions into multiplications, and this is not one of them — M appears only twice. Efficiency cannot be of grave importance anyway, not when the code contains the statement

```
AREA1 = .5 * M * (2 * L);
```

which has two superfluous multiplications (but no divisions!). M can be eliminated. Similarly, N, LMTS, L and AREA1 vanish as the obvious substitutions are made.

We can now remove all those declarations with the strange precisions needed for intermediate results. The remaining declarations consist of just two different types. A close look reveals that K is not declared, even though all other arithmetic variables are. By default K will be FIXED BINARY so a number of type conversions will occur, to no advantage. K should be included in the declarations.

With all the extraneous assignments removed, it is easier to see the underlying structure. It is also easy to see that the indentations reflect little of what is going on. But what is the purpose of the variable I? It is laboriously kept equal to J so that OUT can be called at the end of the last iteration. Clearly I is not needed, for J could be used for the test. But the test is not needed; OUT could be called just after the inner DO loop has terminated. But OUT need not be called at all, for its code could just as well appear in the one place it is invoked. The structure simplifies remarkably.

Now we can see that the summing variable AREA is supposed to be initialized at the beginning of each loop on K. This is much better practice than clearing it before entering the loop and again at the end of each iteration — in a remote procedure at that. Our major criticism of the procedure OUT is not its existence, since it was there for pedagogical reasons, but that it changes AREA and uses LMTS when it does not have to. Destroying modularity in this fashion, referring to seemingly local variables in unexpected places, is an invitation to future bugs. When code is rearranged, or the use of such non-local variables is changed, errors are almost certain to be introduced.

Putting all our improvements together gives:

```
TRAPZ: PROCEDURE OPTIONS(MAIN);
    DECLARE (J,K) FIXED DECIMAL (2),
             AREA FIXED DECIMAL (8,6);

    PUT SKIP EDIT ('AREA UNDER THE CURVE',
                   'BY THE TRAPEZOIDAL RULE')
                   (X(9), A, SKIP, X(7), A);
    PUT SKIP;

    DO K = 4 TO 10;
       AREA = 0.5/K;

       DO J = 1 TO K-1;
          AREA = AREA + ((J/K)**2)/K;
       END;

       PUT SKIP EDIT ('FOR DELTA X=1/', K, AREA)
                      (X(2), A, F(2), X(6), F(9,6));
    END;
END;
```

The program now reflects how straightforward the calculation really is. (Both the original and our version are quite specialized. See problem 2.4.)

The original program gave correct answers, yet we were able to improve upon it considerably. It is clear that successful operation is no guarantee of a good program. The changes we made were not designed to decrease execution time (which is too short to measure reliably) or to decrease storage utilization (which improved by thirty percent). Had we been concerned with optimization in the usual sense, we would have factored $1/K^3$ out of the AREA calculation.

What then did we improve? Readability, principally, but also locality and simplicity of structure. AREA is initialized just before it is used, not in two widely separated and illogical places. The calculation now proceeds from top to bottom without the pointless excursion to a sub-procedure. The original program was puffed up with needless declarations and expressions, with over-simple computations and over-complex control structure.

Programs are not used once and discarded, nor are they run forever without change. They evolve. The new version of the integration program has a greater likelihood of surviving changes later without acquiring bugs. It assists instead of intimidating those who must maintain it. This will be the goal of all our revisions.

To summarize some of the specific points of this chapter:

(1) Write clearly. If you find your code branching around branches or around single statements, turn relational tests around. For each GOTO, ask if it could be cleanly eliminated. Avoid constructions like Fortran's arithmetic IF that force GOTO's and labels upon you.

(2) Be sparing with temporary variables. The clutter from too many temporaries confuses readers (including you), and may well thwart an optimizing compiler.

(3) Be unambiguous. Add parentheses and alter too-similar identifiers to avoid any possibility of misunderstanding.

(4) Don't build *all* of your own tools: use standard library functions like ABS and AMIN1. If no function exists, write your own as a separate function, and add it to your library. Be sufficiently general that your routine can be used in future applications and by other people.

(5) Make sure conditional tests read clearly. Try speaking them aloud; rearrange unwieldy tests.

POINTS TO PONDER

2.1   In case you think the examples in this chapter are rare, here are a few more fragments for you to practice on. Decide what each does, then improve it.

```
IF A>B THEN DO;
LARGE=A;
GO TO CHECK;
END;
LARGE=B;
CHECK: IF LARGE>C THEN GO TO OUTPUT;
LARGE=C;
OUTPUT: ...
```

```
      IF(ITEM1 .LE. ITEM2)GO TO 3
      IHIGH1=ITEM1
      GO TO 4
3     IHIGH1=ITEM2
4     IF(IHIGH1 .GE. ITEM3)GO TO 5
      IHIGH2=ITEM3
      GO TO 6
5     IHIGH2=IHIGH1
6     ...
```

```
DCL A(8);
GET LIST(A);
DO I=1 TO 8;
  IF ABS(A(I))<ABS(A(I+1)) THEN;
      ELSE BEGIN;
         STORE=A(I);
         A(I)=A(I+1);
         A(I+1)=STORE;
         END;
END;
PUT LIST(A);
```

(Find the bug too.)

```
        IF A = 0 THEN GO TO TESTB;
        GO TO CHECK;
TESTB:  IF B = 0 THEN GO TO TESTC;
        GO TO CHECK;
TESTC:  IF C = 0 THEN GO TO NOMORE;
/*HERE WE TEST FOR COMPLEX ROOTS.          */
CHECK:    ...
```

```
      DIMENSION F(46)
      INTEGER F
      ...
      Q=FLOAT(F(I))/FLOAT(J)
      QTRUNC=FLOAT(F(I)/J)
      IF ((Q-QTRUNC).EQ.0.) GO TO 4
```

(Does it even work on your machine?)

```
      DO 10 K=KK,N
      IF(NAME(I).EQ.NAME(K))GO TO 5
      GO TO 10
   5  WRITE(6,3)NAME(I)
   3  FORMAT(' ',A4)
  10  CONTINUE
```

2.2   How long do you think it would take you to make the following Fortran expression for the root of a quadratic syntactically and semantically correct?

```
      ROOT1 = (-B + SQRT(B**2 - 4AC)/2A
```

Six characters *have* to be added, counting decimal points after floating point literals. Did you use eight on your first try? Which version is easier to read? Do you think knowing the quadratic formula by heart helps or hinders proofreading?

2.3   In the trapezoidal integration program discussed above, suppose you had been assigned the job of writing procedure OUT, while someone else wrote the main procedure. How many things do the two of you have to agree on — names of variables, who initializes what — before you can write OUT as it stands? If each initialized his own variables, and the values to be printed were passed as parameters as in

```
      CALL OUT (K, AREA);
```

how many things do you then have to agree on?

2.4   Consider the effort needed to change both versions of the trapezoidal integration program to deal with an arbitrary function F(X) between arbitrary limits A and B. Which conversion represents an easier task and why?

2.5 The following program counts sentences, words and characters in a text. A slash marks the end of the text. Rewrite it using logical IF's instead of arithmetic IF's. How many labels are now necessary?

```
      INTEGER C,KT,BUFR(72),BLANK,COMMA,SCOL,DASH,SLSH,PEROD,NW,NC,NS
      REAL AWS,ASW
      DATA BLANK,COMMA,SCOL,DASH,SLSH,PEROD/' ',',',';','-','/','.'/,
     * NW,NC,NS,KT,C/0,0,0,73,' '/
  101 FORMAT(1H1,35X,'INPUT TEXT')
  102 FORMAT(72A1)
  103 FORMAT(4X,72A1)
  104 FORMAT(///,26X,'NUMBER OF SENTENCES=',I8,/,19X,'AVERAGE NUMBER OF
     *WORDS/SENTENCE=',F8.2,/20X,'AVERAGE NUMBER OF SYMBOLS/WORD=',F8.2)
      WRITE(6,101)
   10 READ(5,102) BUFR
      WRITE(6,103) BUFR
      KT=KT-72
      IF(C-PEROD) 20,35,20
   20 C=BUFR(KT)
   25 IF(C-PEROD) 40,30,40
   30 NS=NS+1
      NW=NW+1
      KT=KT+3
      IF(KT-72) 35,35,10
   35 C=BUFR(KT)
      IF(C-SLSH) 25,75,25
   40 IF(C-BLANK) 50,45,50
   45 NW=NW+1
      GO TO 70
   50 IF(C-COMMA) 55,70,55
   55 IF(C-SCOL) 60,70,60
   60 IF(C-DASH) 65,70,65
   65 NC=NC+1
   70 KT=KT+1
      IF(KT-72) 20,20,10
   75 AWS=FLOAT(NW)/NS
      ASW=FLOAT(NC)/NW
      WRITE(6,104) NS,AWS,ASW
      CALL EXIT
      END
```

2.6 In the preceding program, what happens if a period occurs in column 71 or 72 of an input card? What happens if more than one blank separates two words? What happens if there are leading or trailing blanks on a line? What happens if a sentence ends with a question mark? What else happens? Rewrite the program to make it less vulnerable.

CHAPTER 3: CONTROL STRUCTURE

A computer program is shaped by its data representation and the statements that determine its flow of control. These define the *structure* of a program. There is no sharp distinction between expression and organization; it is more a question of scope. In the previous chapter we were concerned with the details of expressing each statement well. In this chapter and in the next we will concentrate on matters of style that affect the program as a whole.

The control structures of a language provide the framework of a program. These include decision-making with IF and ELSE; looping with DO and WHILE; statement grouping; and procedures or subroutines and functions. The care with which they are used determines how easy it will be to understand the program in the large — in what order things happen, and what controls what. The transformations we made in Chapter 2, such as removing obviously unnecessary GOTO's and statement labels, are simple examples of the proper use of control flow. In this chapter we will go much further.

The easiest construction is the group of statements — a set of operations that are always done together and in sequence. PL/I provides DO-END and BEGIN-END to delimit groups of statements that belong together. In PL/I, branching around a group of statements with THEN GOTO is a sign of "Fortran-think," a clue that rearrangement is called for.

```
IF PRICE(J) > LOT THEN GO TO X;
/*  REDEFINE LOT IF LOWER PRICE IS FOUND */
LOT = PRICE(J);
/*  STORE LOCATION OF THE LOWEST PRICE */
LOCATION = J;
X:  ...
```

Since PL/I's DO-END permits a group of statements to follow an IF, there is never any need to branch around them. And so there is never any need to invent a label, nor to try and figure out where a GOTO is going, nor to wonder how many ways one can get to a label. Turning "greater than" into "less than or equal to" here lets us introduce a DO-END and eliminate the label and the GOTO. At the same time, we indent to emphasize that the IF controls the two indented lines, and omit the repetitive comments, which obscure the code without conveying information.

31

```
IF PRICE(J) <= LOT THEN DO;
    LOT = PRICE(J);
    LOCATION = J;
END;
```

Fortran provides nothing analogous to DO-END; this is one of its major failings. There is no way to treat a block of statements as a group (after an IF, for instance), except by putting them into a subroutine or branching around them. This leads to tortuous code indeed if the program is at all complicated. Even so, some usages are clearer than others.

```
    IF (TABLE (NO) .GT. HICOM) GO TO 50
    GO TO 20
50  HICOM = TABLE (NO)
    NUMBER = NO
20  CONTINUE
```

This should be replaced by

```
    IF (TABLE(NO) .LE. HICOM) GOTO 20
        HICOM = TABLE(NO)
        NUMBER = NO
20  CONTINUE
```

Again we indent the statements that are skipped over, to show that they are controlled by the IF. Within the limitations of Fortran, this is about the best we can do.

Use DO-END *and indenting*
to delimit groups of statements.

In PL/I, an IF may be followed by an ELSE part, to express the action to be taken if the condition is not true. But consider

```
IF SWFSTCTL = '1'
    THEN GOTO CONTINUE ;
    ELSE DO ;
            DIVCTL = DIV ;        /* INITIALIZE CONTROL */
            SWFSTCTL = '1' ;
        END ;
    CONTINUE :
```

The ELSE is a red herring, serving no purpose here. It should be used only when there are two distinct and mutually exclusive actions depending on one test. If there is only one action, it belongs after the THEN, so that the reason for the action can be stated directly:

```
IF SWFSTCTL ¬= '1' THEN DO;
    DIVCTL = DIV;        /* INITIALIZE CONTROL */
    SWFSTCTL = '1';
END;
```

On the other hand, when there really are two cases, an ELSE should be used:

```
        IF DISCRIM<0 THEN DO;
                            PUT EDIT('COMPLEX ROOTS')(SKIP,A);
                            PUT DATA(A,B,C);
                            GOTO MISS;
                       END;
        ROOT=SQRT(DISCRIM);
        ROOT1=(-B+ROOT)/(2*A);
        ROOT2=(-B-ROOT)/(2*A);
        PUT SKIP DATA(A,B,C,ROOT1,ROOT2);
   MISS: ...
```

The actions after the DO-END are done if and only if the DO-END block is *not* done; they should be part of an ELSE:

```
        IF DISCRIM < 0 THEN DO;
            PUT EDIT ('COMPLEX ROOTS') (SKIP, A);
            PUT DATA (A, B, C);
        END;
        ELSE DO;
            ROOT = SQRT(DISCRIM);
            ROOT1 = (-B+ROOT) / (2*A);
            ROOT2 = (-B-ROOT) / (2*A);
            PUT SKIP DATA (A, B, C, ROOT1, ROOT2);
        END;
```

In Fortran, it is hard to make the structure of an IF-ELSE explicit, since there is no ELSE, and only a single (restricted) statement can follow the IF. For even more complicated combinations, things get tough indeed. Consider this fragment for keeping track of the largest and smallest A(I):

```
        IF(A(I).LE.BIG) GO TO 100
        BIG=A(I)
        GO TO 49
    100 IF(A(I).GE.SMAL) GO TO 49
        SMAL=A(I)
     49 CONTINUE
```

This is an essentially mechanical translation of the algorithm into Fortran, and as such is hard to fault. It is possible, however, to write the code rather more clearly in this special case:

```
        IF (A(I) .GT. BIG) BIG = A(I)
        IF (A(I) .LT. SMAL) SMAL = A(I)
```

If the first test succeeds, the second presumably cannot, but an occasional redundant test is a small price to pay for improved readability.

By the way, it is necessary to be quite careful when tests might overlap. Avoid situations like this one:

```
        IF HRS_WORKED<=40
            THEN CALL REGPAY;
        IF HRS_WORKED>=40
            THEN CALL OTPAY;
```

People who work exactly forty hours are rewarded with a double paycheck! An IF-ELSE divides things into two separate pieces, only *one* of which is done. It also ensures that someone reading the code can see that only one thing is done. Thus:

```
IF HRS_WORKED <= 40 THEN
    CALL REGPAY;
ELSE
    CALL OTPAY;
```

Use IF-ELSE *to emphasize that
only one of two actions is to be performed.*

Another major aspect of control flow is looping. We are already familiar with the indexed loop, the

```
DO I = 1 TO N
```

of PL/I and the

```
DO 10 I = 1, N
```

of Fortran. But even more frequent are loops which are not arithmetic progressions, as in this sorting procedure:

```
SORT: PROCEDURE OPTIONS(MAIN);
      DECLARE  (NAMES(50),SPARE)CHARACTER(10),
      SWITCH BIT(1),(I,N) FIXED BINARY;
      /*READ IN ALL 50 NAMES                        */
      GET LIST(NAMES);
      N=50;
AGAIN:SWITCH='0'B;                      /*CLEAR THE SWITCH*/
      DO I=1 TO N-1;         /*SET THE NUMBER OF COMPARISONS*/
         IF NAMES(I)>NAMES(I+1) THEN    /*SWAP THE PAIR   */
            DO;                         /*USING SPARE,AND */
               SWITCH='1'B;            /*  SET THE SWITCH*/
               SPARE=NAMES(I);
               NAMES(I)=NAMES(I+1);
               NAMES(I+1)=SPARE;
            END;
      END;
      N=N-1;                  /*DECREASE NUMBER OF  COMPARISONS*/
      IF SWITCH THEN GOTO AGAIN; /*REPEAT IF SWAP WAS MADE*/
      PUT LIST(NAMES);
   END;
```

There are actually two loops here, although it takes a bit of work to find that out. The inner loop is clear enough; it runs from 1 to N-1. The outer loop is executed so long as an interchange has been made during a pass through the list of items. This is recorded by SWITCH, which is '1'B if an exchange has been made, and '0'B otherwise.

The PL/I DO-WHILE statement provides a way to write this loop that makes it instantly obvious to the reader that there *is* a loop, and what controls it.

```
SORT: PROCEDURE OPTIONS (MAIN);
   DECLARE (NAMES(50), SPARE) CHARACTER(10);
   DECLARE SWITCH BIT(1);
   DECLARE YES BIT(1) INITIAL ('1'B), NO BIT(1) INITIAL ('0'B);
   DECLARE (I, N) FIXED BINARY;

   GET LIST (NAMES);
   SWITCH = YES;
   DO N = 50 TO 2 BY -1 WHILE (SWITCH = YES);
      SWITCH = NO;
      DO I = 1 TO N-1;
         IF NAMES(I) > NAMES(I+1) THEN DO;
            SWITCH = YES;
            SPARE = NAMES(I);
            NAMES(I) = NAMES(I+1);
            NAMES(I+1) = SPARE;
         END;
      END;
   END;
   PUT LIST (NAMES);
END;
```

The original version used a label and an IF-GOTO to build the outer loop, and a DO for the inner; it was hard to see at a glance that there are truly two loops or where each begins. Now the two loops are explicitly marked as such.

We have also used the variables YES and NO instead of the literals '1'B and '0'B, to make the code read a bit more clearly.

As much as possible, a program should be written so the control flow structures lead the reader quickly and directly to an understanding of what the program does. For example, in

```
A:   IF COUNT(RANK) < 4 THEN
     BEGIN;
        PUT LIST(RECONVERT(RANK));
        COUNT(RANK) = COUNT(RANK) + 1;
        GOTO A;
     END;
```

the construction

```
IF ... THEN BEGIN ... END
```

is a clear signal that the group of statements between BEGIN and END is to be done exactly once if the condition is true, or not at all if it is false; then, in either case, execution will resume after the END. But look carefully, and you will find that the last statement of the group is a branch back to the test. Although the code claims to be merely an IF, that is a lie — it is actually a loop.

A DO-WHILE provides an honest way to say what the code does:

```
DO WHILE (COUNT(RANK) < 4);
   PUT LIST(RECONVERT(RANK));
   COUNT(RANK) = COUNT(RANK) + 1;
END;
```

The advantage is not that the second version is smaller, but that it is explicit. The DO-WHILE says "This is a loop," and is that much easier to understand. The first version forces the reader to ferret out the control flow.

The WHILE statement, which specifies a loop with an arbitrary termination condition (tested at the top), is not available in Fortran. This means that loops in Fortran are often contorted into DO loops, which makes them hard to understand and prone to errors. Alternatively, loops are written with IF's and GOTO's, which conceal the structure of code, again making it hard to understand and prone to errors. Newer languages have better control-flow constructs, like PL/I's DO-WHILE. But the DO-WHILE is seldom used, and PL/I programmers often write much as their Fortran colleagues do.

Use DO *and* DO-WHILE *to emphasize
the presence of loops.*

Things get more complicated when several fundamental structures are intertwined and built with spare parts instead of being spelled out explicitly, as in this excerpt from a procedure that computes bowling scores.

```
          Y=0; L=1; FRM=1;
     CYCLE:    IF X(L) = 10 THEN    STRK: DO;
                                          Y=Y+10+X(L+1)+X(L+2);
                                          L=L+1;
                                          GO TO NEXT;
                                          END STRK;
               IF X(L) + X(L+1) = 10 THEN    SPR: DO;
                                          Y=Y+10+X(L+1);
                                          L=L+2;
                                          GO TO NEXT;
                                          END SPR;
                              ELSE    REG: DO;
                                          Y=Y+X(L)+X(L+1);
                                          L=L+2;
                                          GO TO NEXT;
                                          END REG;
     NEXT: IF FRM=10 THEN RETURN(Y);
          FRM=FRM+1;    GO TO CYCLE;
```

There are actually two structures here, both built with IF's and GOTO's instead of with the higher-level facilities provided by PL/I. The outer part is an indexed loop, represented by

```
                    FRM=1;
     CYCLE:
            ...
     NEXT: IF FRM=10 THEN RETURN(Y);
          FRM=FRM+1;    GO TO CYCLE;
```

and the interior is a three-way decision: strike, spare, or regular frame.

Rewritten with explicit control structures, it becomes much clearer. Bowlers will appreciate the correction of the computation for a spare; non-bowlers may be less interested.

```
         Y = 0;
         L = 1;
         DO FRM = 1 TO 10;
            IF X(L) = 10 THEN DO;                  /* STRIKE */
               Y = Y + 10 + X(L+1) + X(L+2);
               L = L + 1;
            END;
            ELSE IF X(L) + X(L+1) = 10 THEN DO;    /* SPARE */
               Y = Y + 10 + X(L+2);
               L = L + 2;
            END;
            ELSE DO;                    /* REGULAR */
               Y = Y + X(L) + X(L+1);
               L = L + 2;
            END;
         END;
         RETURN(Y);
```

(There is another version of this program in Chapter 8.)

As a fringe benefit, the RETURN statement now occurs at the end, where one would normally expect it, instead of being buried inside. It is a good rule of thumb that a program should read from top to bottom in the order that it will be executed; if this is not true, watch out for the bugs that often accompany poor structure.

Make your programs read from top to bottom.

The code we used to express the three-way decision in the bowling program is an example of an important control construction, the multi-way decision, sometimes called a CASE statement. Some languages provide a separate statement for writing such branches; in PL/I, multi-way decisions are usually best expressed as a chain of IF ... ELSE IF ... ELSE, like this:

```
IF condition-1 THEN
   statement-1
ELSE IF condition-2 THEN
   statement-2
...
ELSE IF condition-n THEN
   statement-n
ELSE
   default-statement
```

The *condition*'s are read from top to bottom; at the first *condition* that is satisfied, the *statement* that follows is executed, and then the entire construct is exited. The *statement* parts may be single statements, or (as above) a group of statements enclosed in DO-END. The last ELSE handles the "default" situation, i.e., where none of the other alternatives was chosen. This trailing ELSE part may be omitted if the program logic requires no action for the default, although leaving it in with an error message may help to catch "impossible" conditions.

We will return in a moment to how to handle the CASE statement in Fortran.

Note that we align all of the ELSE's in a CASE, rather than lining up each ELSE with the corresponding IF. This emphasizes that all the legs of the CASE have equal status and keeps them from marching off the right side of the page.

Use IF ... ELSE IF ... ELSE IF ... ELSE ...
to implement multi-way branches.

The CASE statement is often recognizable in a sequence of related decisions, where only minor rearrangement is needed to bring things into the proper form:

```
IF AMT_OF_SALES <= 50.00 THEN COMM = 00.00;
IF AMT_OF_SALES > 50.00 THEN IF AMT_OF_SALES <= 100.00
    THEN COMM = .02 * AMT_OF_SALES;
IF AMT_OF_SALES > 100.00 THEN
    COMM = .03 * AMT_OF_SALES;
```

The two IF's in the second line can certainly be compressed into a single test with the logical operator &. So an improved version might read

```
IF AMT_OF_SALES <= 50.00 THEN
    COMM = 00.00;
IF AMT_OF_SALES > 50.00 & AMT_OF_SALES <= 100.00 THEN
    COMM = 0.02 * AMT_OF_SALES;
IF AMT_OF_SALES > 100.00 THEN
    COMM = 0.03 * AMT_OF_SALES;
```

But the tests in an ELSE-IF chain are done in the prescribed order, and this fact may be used to advantage. If it fails the first test, AMT_OF_SALES is greater than 50; if it fails the second, it is greater than 100. Neither test need be repeated if an ELSE-IF is used:

```
IF AMT_OF_SALES <= 50.00 THEN
    COMM = 00.00;
ELSE IF AMT_OF_SALES <= 100.00 THEN
    COMM = 0.02 * AMT_OF_SALES;
ELSE
    COMM = 0.03 * AMT_OF_SALES;
```

Peeling off cases in numerical order in this way is also highly readable and easy to change.

We have now mentioned several control flow constructions:

statement grouping with, for example, DO-END or BEGIN-END;

decision making with IF-ELSE;

looping with DO and DO-WHILE;

subroutines, functions, or procedures.

The DO loop comes in at least two flavors in PL/I, indexed and DO-WHILE, and the IF-ELSE can be extended into the CASE or multi-way decision.

Taken together, this set of constructions is generally adequate for comfortably expressing any sequencing operations in a program. The term "structured programming" is sometimes used (at least in a narrow sense) to refer to the process of programming with nothing but proper nests of these basic operations.

The advantage of this discipline is that since there are no GOTO statements, it is generally easier to follow the flow of control; for the most part such a program reads directly from top to bottom, so the reader doesn't have to follow paths with his fingers all over the listing. And no GOTO's means no labels — there is only one way to reach each statement.

On the other hand, structured programming in this limited sense certainly will not solve all your programming problems. We will see in the rest of this chapter plenty of code that contains only the basic constructions in properly nested combinations, yet which is hard to understand and even incorrect.

Use the fundamental control flow constructs.

Bare Fortran doesn't have any of these fundamental structures. What can you do to cope? We have several suggestions. For the long term, the 1977 Fortran Standard provides an ELSE and a way to group statements after IF and ELSE; it looks like:

```
IF (condition) THEN
     statements
ELSE
     statements
ENDIF
```

These can be nested, and there can be an ELSE IF. Regrettably, Fortran 77 does not have a WHILE statement. There is also a version of the debugging compiler WATFIV, called WATFIV-S, which supports statement grouping, ELSE, and WHILE.

A second possibility, which may be more accessible in the short run, is to use one of the host of Fortran preprocessors which have been developed in the past few years. A preprocessor is a program which translates a Fortran dialect with adequate control flow statements into pure Fortran; ideally you never need to look at the generated Fortran. (The "pseudo-code" that we will present in the next sections is based on Ratfor, a language implemented by one such Fortran preprocessor. It is described in *Software Tools*, by Brian W. Kernighan and P. J. Plauger, Addison-Wesley, 1976.)

A third possibility is to think out your code in a decent language, then translate into Fortran when it comes time to start transcribing the code into machine-readable form. This requires no software, just discipline. To see how it works in practice, consider the following quadratic equation solver, in which IF statements come so thick and fast as to baffle the reader.

```
C       OBTAINS SOLUTIONS OF THE EQUATION A*X**2 + B*X + C = 0
C
   10 READ(5,8000) A,B,C
 8000 FORMAT(3F10.5)
C       A IN COLUMNS 1-10, B IN COLUMNS 11-20, C IN COLUMNS 21-30
      WRITE(6,9000) A,B,C
 9000 FORMAT(4H0A = F12.5,3X,3HB = ,F12.5,3X,3HC = ,F12.5)
C       TEST FOR TWO ZEROS
      IF(B.EQ.0..AND.C.EQ.0.)  GO TO 15
C       AT THIS POINT EITHER B, OR C, OR BOTH MAY BE NONZERO
      IF(B.NE.0..AND.C.NE.0.)  GO TO 50
C       AT THIS POINT EITHER B IS 0 OR C IS ZERO
      IF(A)  30,20,30
   15 IF(A.EQ.0.) STOP
   20 WRITE(6,9010)
 9010 FORMAT(33H TRIVIAL CASE. TWO OR MORE ZEROS.)
      GO TO 10
C       NOW TEST FOR C = 0 CASE.
   30 IF(C)  60,40,60
   40 XA = B/A
      XB = 0.
      GO TO 100
   50 IF(A.NE.0.)  GO TO 60
      XA = -C/B
      XB = 0.
      GO TO 100
C       START OF MAIN COMPUTATION
   60 Q = B*B-4.*A*C
      XX = -B/(2.*A)
      IF(Q)  80,70,80
   70 XA = XX
      XB = XX
      GO TO 100
   80 QA = ABS(Q)
      XS = SQRT(QA)/(2.*A)
      IF(Q)  110,110,90
   90 XA = XX + XS
      XB = XX - XS
  100 WRITE(6,9020) XA,XB
 9020 FORMAT(5H X1 = ,F12.5,3X,4HX2 = ,F12.5)
      GO TO 10
  110 XA = XS
      XB = -XS
      WRITE(6,9030) XX,XA,XX,XB
 9030 FORMAT(5H X1 = ,F12.5,2H + ,F12.5,2H I,5X,4HX2 = ,F12.5,2H +,
     1 F12.5,2H I)
      GO TO 10
      END
```

A painful trace through the logic reveals several small errors. The most significant is statement 40, the case where only C is zero, which should have a minus sign:

```
   40 XA = -B/A
```

Statement 20 writes "TRIVIAL CASE. TWO OR MORE ZEROS.", even though the case where all three coefficients are zero is eliminated by the STOP at statement 15. Worse, the same message is delivered for the equations

`A*X**2` = 0, a valid equation with a double root at zero.

`B*X` = 0, which has a single root at zero.

`C` = 0, which is true only when `C` is zero.

Trivial they may be, but all are different and two out of the three are legitimate. Finally, for the case where only A is zero, the program prints out two roots, `-C/B` and 0.0, even though the equation has only one root.

A useful way to write a complex program in any language, not just Fortran, is to code it first in a convenient, expressive pseudo-language (typically *not* Fortran or PL/I) and then, when it appears correct, to translate it into the language at hand (Fortran in this case). At the highest level, we might even write something like

```
REPEAT
    read and print coefficients A, B and C
    solve quadratic Ax² + Bx + C
```

REPEAT implies an indefinitely repeated loop. On each iteration we fetch a new set of coefficients and solve the corresponding quadratic.

The next step is to fill in some details, a process sometimes called "top-down design" or "successive refinement." (We will have more to say about this in Chapter 4.) Solving the quadratic is a multi-way decision, to decide what specific kind of quadratic must be dealt with. Thus the second version is

```
REPEAT
    read and print A, B, C
    IF (A = 0 & B = 0 & C = 0)
       stop
    ELSE IF (A = 0 & B = 0)
       equation is C = 0
    ELSE IF (A = 0)
       only root is -C/B
    ELSE IF (C = 0)
       roots are -B/A and 0
    ELSE
       Realpart = -B/(2A)
       Discrim = B**2 - 4AC
       Imagpart = sqrt(abs(Discrim))/(2A)
       IF (Discrim >= 0)
          roots are Realpart+Imagpart and Realpart-Imagpart
       ELSE
          roots are (Realpart, Imagpart) and (Realpart, -Imagpart)
```

Indeed this is no language in particular, but it is sufficiently precise for our needs, and readily understood. There is no need for more formality. Not only is the pseudo-code readable and precise, but it is sufficiently close to normal programming languages that we can apply principles of programming style to it just as if it were executable. We can even check that it works, in the sense of doing the right things at the right times.

Once we are satisfied, we translate. Since most Fortrans do not allow grouping of statements, let alone a PL/I-like `IF-ELSE`, we must link up the pieces of the `IF-ELSE` structures by `GOTO`'s. At the same time we can fix minor details like output formats and statement labels, and make the variable names more mnemonic.

The resulting code is:

```
C   OBTAINS SOLUTIONS OF THE EQUATION A*X**2 + B*X + C = 0
C
    10 READ(5,11) A, B, C
    11     FORMAT (3F10.0)
       WRITE(6,12) A, B, C
    12     FORMAT ('0A =', 1PE16.6, ', B =', 1PE16.6, ', C =', 1PE16.6)
       IF (A .EQ. 0.0 .AND. B .EQ. 0.0 .AND. C .EQ. 0) STOP
       IF (A .NE. 0.0 .OR. B .NE. 0.0) GOTO 20
          WRITE(6,13) C
    13        FORMAT (' EQUATION SAYS', 1PE16.6,' = 0')
          GOTO 90
    20 IF (A .NE. 0.0) GOTO 30
          R1 = -C/B
          WRITE(6,21) R1
    21        FORMAT (' ONE ROOT. R =', 1PE16.6)
          GOTO 90
C A IS NOT ZERO
    30 IF (C .NE. 0.0) GOTO 40
          R1 = -B/A
          R2 = 0.0
          WRITE(6,31) R1, R2
    31        FORMAT (' R1 =', 1PE16.6, ', R2 =', 1PE16.6)
          GOTO 90
C GENERAL CASE: A, C NON-ZERO
    40 RREAL = -B/(2.0*A)
          DISC = B**2 - 4.0*A*C
          RIMAG = SQRT(ABS(DISC))/(2.0*A)
          IF (DISC .LT. 0.0) GOTO 50
          R1 = RREAL + RIMAG
          R2 = RREAL - RIMAG
          WRITE(6,31) R1, R2
          GOTO 90
    50 R1 = -RIMAG
          WRITE(6,51) RREAL, RIMAG, RREAL, R1
    51        FORMAT (' R1 = (', 1PE16.6, ',', 1PE16.6, ')',
       $             ', R2 = (', 1PE16.6, ',', 1PE16.6, ')')
    90 GOTO 10
       END
```

Two roots are printed only when there are two, one is printed when and only when there is one, and an imaginary part is printed only when called for. More important, it is easy to determine how the program gets to each separate case. (This program is still far from being a general-purpose quadratic-equation solver; the defenses needed against every conceivable numerical hazard require more analysis than we can go into here.)

Write first in an easy-to-understand pseudo-language;
then translate into whatever language you have to use.

IF-ELSE constructions formed the framework of our quadratic routine, as they do in most programs. But mere use of IF-ELSE does not guarantee that the result will stand up. Consider this fragment, which computes the effective weight of an airplane, based on its true weight, length, and wingspan.

```
IF LENGTH >= 30 & LENGTH <= 50 THEN

    IF WING < .6*LENGTH THEN WEIGHT1 =
        (1+.08-.037)*WEIGHT;

    ELSE WEIGHT1=(1+.08+.045)*WEIGHT;
ELSE   IF LENGTH > 50 & LENGTH < 60 THEN

        IF WING < .6*LENGTH THEN
            WEIGHT1=(1+.09-.037)*
            WEIGHT; ·

        ELSE WEIGHT1=(1+.09+.045)*
            WEIGHT;

    ELSE   IF LENGTH > 60 & LENGTH
            < 80 THEN

        IF   WING < .6*LENGTH THEN
            WEIGHT1=(1+.105-.037)*
            WEIGHT;

    ELSE WEIGHT1=(1+.105+.045)*
            WEIGHT;

        ELSE IF WING < .6*LENGTH
            THEN

            WEIGHT1=(1+.122-
            .037)*WEIGHT;
            ELSE WEIGHT1=(1+
            .122+.045)*WEIGHT;
```

When a program is well-structured, its layout can be made clean. For instance, programs that avoid labels and undisciplined branches should use indentation to emphasize the logical structure. (This program was originally displayed with vertical bars joining IF's with their corresponding ELSE's.) But indentation is no substitute for organization; tasteful formatting and top-to-bottom flow is no guarantee that the code cannot be improved.

Look at all the repetitions. The entire structure is turned inside out. If the test on WING is done first and the result saved for later use, and if we remove all the redundant tests, the code simplifies remarkably. Rearrangement also reveals the oversight in the original: the case where LENGTH is exactly 60 has been lumped in with the case for 80 and larger.

```
IF WING < 0.6 * LENGTH THEN
    CORR = 1.0 - 0.037;
ELSE
    CORR = 1.0 + 0.045;

IF LENGTH >= 80 THEN
    WEIGHT1 = (CORR+0.122) * WEIGHT;
ELSE IF LENGTH > 60 THEN
    WEIGHT1 = (CORR+0.105) * WEIGHT;
ELSE IF LENGTH > 50 THEN
    WEIGHT1 = (CORR+0.09) * WEIGHT;
ELSE IF LENGTH >= 30 THEN
    WEIGHT1 = (CORR+0.08) * WEIGHT;
```

Both versions use a nest of IF-ELSE's, but ours uses it in a special way: we never use an IF immediately after a THEN, but only after an ELSE. The result is much easier to understand, because we know that exactly one case is done (if LENGTH exceeds 30), and it is clear how we get to it: it is the first condition satisfied as we read down the list of ELSE IF's. After one of these has been done, execution resumes after the entire statement. Of course this is just a CASE statement.

The construction THEN IF is often a warning that trouble looms ahead.

```
IF QTY > 10 THEN                                          /*A*/
    IF QTY > 200 THEN                                     /*B*/
        IF QTY >= 500 THEN BILL_A = BILL_A + 1.00;        /*C*/
                     ELSE BILL_A = BILL_A + .50;          /*C*/
                ELSE;                                     /*B*/
        ELSE BILL_A = .00;                                /*A*/
```

Those letters down the right hand side are designed to help you figure out what is going on, but as usual, no amount of commenting can rescue bad code. The sequence of THEN-IF's requires you to maintain a mental pushdown stack of what tests were made, so that at the appropriate point you can pop them until you determine the corresponding action (if you can still remember). You might time yourself as you determine what this code does when QTY equals 350. How about 150?

Since at most one of a set of actions is ever called for here, what we really want is some form of CASE statement. Changing the order in which the decisions are made leads to a clearer version:

```
IF QTY >= 500 THEN
    BILL_A = BILL_A + 1.00;
ELSE IF QTY > 200 THEN
    BILL_A = BILL_A + 0.50;
ELSE IF QTY <= 10 THEN
    BILL_A = 0.0;
```

Now all we need do is read down the list of tests until we find one that is met, read across to the corresponding action, and continue after the last ELSE.

In Fortran, this could be rendered as

```
IF (QTY .GE. 500.0) BILLA = BILLA + 1.0
IF (QTY .LT. 500.0 .AND. QTY .GT. 200.0) BILLA = BILLA + 0.5
IF (QTY .LE. 10.0) BILLA = 0.0
```

which is best if the tests are mutually exclusive and if the relations and actions are

simple enough to write one per line. Don't let anyone tell you this is not efficient —
it doesn't take all that much time to make the whole set of tests, and you're more
likely to get the code right the first time. If it does take too much time, and you
have measurements that prove it, then and only then should you re-write it with
GOTO's.

The THEN-IF was the culprit in this example, but there is another symptom of
the same problem. Note the null ELSE clause in the original, required to make the
unstacking of the nested IF's come out right when one of the conditions has no
corresponding action. These seemingly useless statements cauterize the stumps of
any ill-thought-out THEN-IF's buried in the code. A program containing null ELSE
clauses is suspect, if for no other reason than that it was written by someone burned
by THEN-IF's often enough to sprinkle null ELSE's around for insurance.

The THEN-IF does have its uses. It is often the only way to ensure that tests
are performed in the proper order, as in

```
IF I > 0 THEN
    IF A(I) = B(I) THEN ...
```

which checks that I is in range before it is used as an index. Some languages provide special AND's and OR's which guarantee left-to-right evaluation and early exit as
soon as the truth value of the expression is determined. But if you are not fortunate enough to be able to program with these useful tools, wrap a DO-END around
the inner IF so you don't have to worry about trailing ELSE's.

Avoid THEN-IF *and null* ELSE.

Consider this procedure for finding the largest of a set of positive numbers:

```
FINDNUM: PROC OPTIONS (MAIN);
         DCL NEWIN DEC FLOAT (4);
             LARGE DEC FLOAT (4) INIT (.0E1);
             /* .0 x 10**1 = .0 x 10 = 0.0                    */
NEXT_C:  GET LIST (NEWIN);
         IF NEWIN >=0
             THEN IF NEWIN > LARGE
                         THEN LARGE = NEWIN;
                         ELSE GO TO NEXT_C;
             ELSE GO TO FINISH;
         GO TO NEXT_C;
FINISH:  PUT LIST (LARGE);
         END;
```

Change the illegal semicolon into a comma in the second line. Ignore the curious
zero in the INIT attribute, and the equally curious explanatory comment. Now, try
to trace the flow of control. This is not a trivial exercise. How does one get to that
last GO TO NEXT_C, for example? Why, from the innermost THEN clause, of
course.

An ELSE GOTO tells you where you went if you didn't do the THEN, leaving you
momentarily at a loss in finding the successor to the THEN clause. And when ELSE
GOTO's are used one after the other, as here, the mind boggles. Needless to say,

ELSE RETURN is no better.

Such convolutions are almost never necessary if decisions are made in the right order.

```
FINDNUM: PROCEDURE OPTIONS (MAIN);
   DECLARE (NEWIN, LARGE) DECIMAL FLOAT (4);
   NEWIN = 0;
   LARGE = 0;
   DO WHILE (NEWIN >= 0);
      GET LIST (NEWIN);
      IF NEWIN > LARGE THEN
         LARGE = NEWIN;
   END;
   PUT LIST (LARGE);
END;
```

What we have here is a simple DO-WHILE, done while the number read is not negative, controlling a simple IF-THEN. Of course we have rearranged the order of testing, but the end-of-data marker chosen was a convenient one and does not interfere with the principal work of the routine. True, our version makes one extra test, comparing the marker against LARGE, but that will hardly affect the overall efficiency of the sequence. Readability is certainly improved by avoiding the ELSE GOTO's.

Avoid ELSE GOTO *and* ELSE RETURN.

Most of the IF-ELSE examples we have shown so far have a characteristic in common. Each approximates, as closely as the programmer could manage, a minimum depth decision tree for the problem at hand. If all outcomes have equal probability, such a tree arrives at the appropriate action with the minimum number of tests on the average, so it might seem desirable to lay out programs accordingly. But a program is a one-dimensional construct, which obscures any two-dimensional connectedness it may have. The minimum depth tree is not the best structure for a readable program.

Recall the program for finding the minimum of three numbers which we showed at the beginning of Chapter 2. Let us rewrite that program in PL/I, adhering to the spirit of the original Fortran, but using only IF-ELSE's:

```
IF X >= Y THEN
   IF Y >= Z THEN
      SMALL = Z;
   ELSE
      SMALL = Y;
ELSE
   IF X >= Z THEN
      SMALL = Z;
   ELSE
      SMALL = X;
```

Even though neatly laid out and systematically indented, it is still not easy to grasp. Not all the confusion of the original can be attributed to the welter of GOTO's and statement numbers. What we have here is a "bushy" tree, needlessly complex in any event, but still hard to read simply because it is conceptually short and fat.

The ELSE-IF sequence, on the other hand, is long and skinny as trees go; it seems to more closely reflect how we think. (Note that our revised minimum function was also linear.) It is easier to read down a list of items, considering them one at a time, than to remember the complete path to some interior part of a tree, even if the path has only two or three links. Seldom is it actually necessary to repeat tests in the process of stringing out a tree into a list; often it is just a matter of performing the tests in a judicious order. Yet too often programmers tend to build a thicket of logic where a series of signposts are called for.

Let us summarize our discussion of IF-ELSE. The most important principle is to avoid bushy decision trees like

```
IF  ... THEN
    IF ... THEN
    ELSE ...
ELSE
    IF ... THEN
    ELSE ...
```

The bushy tree should almost always be reorganized into a CASE statement, which is implemented as a string of ELSE-IF's in PL/I and as a series of IF's linked with GOTO's in Fortran. The resulting long thin tree is much easier to understand.

A THEN-IF is an early warning that a decision tree is growing the wrong way. A null ELSE indicates that the programmer knows that trouble lies ahead and is trying to defend against it. An ELSE GOTO from such a structure may leave the reader at a loss to understand how the following statement is reached. A null THEN or (more commonly) THEN GOTO usually indicates that a relational test needs to be turned around, and some set of statements made into a group with DO-END.

The general rule is: after you make a decision, *do something*. Don't just go somewhere or make another decision. If you follow each decision by the action that goes with it, you can see at a glance what each decision implies.

Follow each decision as closely as possible
with its associated action.

We turn now to the general area of data structure and representation. A program frequently turns out ill-formed or hard to work with because its data representation is inappropriate for the job at hand. We have already seen one small example of this: the change from LOGICAL to INTEGER variables clarified the dating service program of Chapter 2.

Choosing the right data types is usually pretty simple in Fortran, for there are few choices — basically just INTEGER, LOGICAL, and REAL. In PL/I, however, there are many more choices, and accordingly more ways to go wrong. Here is an example where data structure makes all the difference. It is from a program which makes change for an amount DIFF dollars, using $20 bills and smaller denominations. The example is supposed to handle positive values of DIFF up to $10,000;

the part we have omitted deals with negative and zero values.

```
        DECLARE A(8) REAL DECIMAL FIXED(6,2) INITIAL(20.,10.,5.,1.,.25,
        .1,.05,.01),(AMT_PD,DIFF,COST) REAL DECIMAL FIXED(8,2),
        (I,J,NT) REAL DECIMAL FIXED(3);
    ...

        CHANGE:DO I=1 TO 8;
            NT=0;
            CASH:DO J=1 TO 50;

    /* IN THIS LOOP WE DETERMINE THE MAXIMUM NUMBERS OF TIMES THE
        DIFFERENCE IS DIVISIBLE BY THE I(TH) DENOMINATION      */

            IF DIFF/(J*A(I))<1 THEN GO TO OUT;
            NT=J;
        END CASH;
    /*  WE THEN DECREASE THE DIFFERENCE BY THE APPROPRIATE AMOUNT
        AND PRINT THE APPROPRIATE STATEMENT           */

        OUT:IF NT>0 THEN DO;
            DIFF=DIFF-NT*A(I);
            IF I=1 THEN
                PUT SKIP(2) LIST(NT,'TWENTY DOLLAR BILLS');
            IF I=2 THEN
                PUT SKIP(2) LIST(NT,'TEN DOLLAR BILLS');
            IF I=3 THEN
                PUT SKIP(2) LIST(NT,'FIVE DOLLAR BILLS');
            IF I=4 THEN
                PUT SKIP(2) LIST(NT,'ONE DOLLAR BILLS');
            IF I=5 THEN
                PUT SKIP(2) LIST(NT,'QUARTERS');
            IF I=6 THEN
                PUT SKIP(2) LIST(NT,'DIMES');
            IF I=7 THEN
                PUT SKIP(2) LIST(NT,'NICKELS');
            IF I=8 THEN
                PUT SKIP(2) LIST(NT,'PENNIES');
        END CHANGE;
```

Consider the variable NT. It always has the value J−1 whenever it is referenced; it is not needed. Worse, its presence helps obscure an important point — the algorithm is wrong.

The inner DO loop (at label CASH) is clearly designed to exit via the IF before the loop completes. But 50 times $20 is only $1000, not $10,000, so an exit can occur from the bottom of the loop. The program will make change poorly at or over $1020, and incorrectly over $1820.50.

Whenever a DO loop is designed "never" to exit from the bottom, one should ask:

(1) Are there any circumstances when an exit from the bottom might take place?

(2) What happens if such an exit does occur?

The first question points to the typo that made the upper limit of the CASH loop 50 instead of 500; the second question reveals that the program charges straight on after an error. (A judiciously placed error message, plus a comprehensive set of test cases, would have brought this bug to light before it became a bad example.)

You might ask if it's fair to criticize such a "typographical" error, as we have done several times. Our answer is that, regrettably, a program with a typo in it won't work. If you're lucky, it will fail to compile. Worse, like this one, it may run but provide subtly wrong answers.

One flaw in a program is often a clue that more are present. The whole purpose of the strange computation in the CASH loop is to determine the maximum number of times the I-th denomination A(I) can be removed from DIFF without causing overdraw. This is exactly what division does. In fact, DIFF/A(I) gives the desired result when truncated to the next lower integer, and the built-in function FLOOR performs just such a truncation. The CASH loop is not only incorrect, but wasteful and unnecessary.

Let us reconsider the data representation. It hardly seems necessary to rattle down a series of IF's to output the appropriate denomination name. If instead we use indexing, we can rewrite the fragment as:

```
DECLARE NAME(8) CHARACTER(19) INITIAL (
    'TWENTY DOLLAR BILLS', 'TEN DOLLAR BILLS   ',
    'FIVE DOLLAR BILLS  ', 'ONE DOLLAR BILLS   ',
    'QUARTERS           ', 'DIMES              ',
    'NICKELS            ', 'PENNIES            ');
DECLARE DENOM(8) REAL DECIMAL FIXED (6,2)
    INITIAL (20.00, 10.00, 5.00, 1.00, 0.25, 0.10, 0.05, 0.01);
DECLARE NT REAL DECIMAL FIXED (3);
DECLARE DIFF REAL DECIMAL FIXED (8,2);
...

DO I = 1 TO 8;
    NT = FLOOR(DIFF/DENOM(I));
    DIFF = MOD(DIFF, DENOM(I));
    IF NT > 0 THEN
        PUT SKIP(2) LIST (NT, NAME(I));
END;
```

The different denomination names are collected into a character-string array **NAME** so we can use the computed index NT to select the one to print. NT now performs a useful function and so is retained. Not only is this version smaller and more readable, but it works correctly for any positive value that DIFF can assume. (We have not shown the code for the case when DIFF is negative or zero.)

It is interesting that this program failed to use truncating division when it should have, while the very first example in Chapter 1 used it to excess. In either case, the result is obscure code. Some friendly criticism could have helped each toward a happier middle ground. Curiously, manuscripts are almost always reviewed before publication, yet programs are most often inspected only by the original coder and the compiler. Both have blind spots.

Use data arrays to avoid repetitive control sequences.

It is easy to overlook a poor choice of data representation by getting involved in fixing up the intricate code that usually accompanies it. The following program reads cards and centers the non-blank information on each card within a border of periods.

```
      DIMENSION STRING(80),PHRASE(80)
      BLANK = 1H
      PERIOD = 1H.
  999 READ 100, (PHRASE(I),I=1,80)
  100 FORMAT(80A1)
  103 FORMAT(1H0)
C
C     LOOP 1
C
      NBEF=0
      J =1
    1 IF(PHRASE(J).NE.BLANK) GO TO 2
      NBEF=NBEF+1
      J = J+1
      IF(J.EQ.81) GO TO 1000
      GO TO 1
C
C     LOOP 2
C
    2 NAFT=0
      I=80
    3 IF(PHRASE(I).NE.BLANK)GO TO 4
      NAFT=NAFT+1
      I=I-1
      GO TO 3
C
C     COMPUTE LENGTHS OF PHRASE AND MARGIN
C
    4 LENGTH=80-(NBEF+NAFT)
      MARGIN = (80-LENGTH)/2+1
      IND1=NBEF
      IND2=MARGIN
      DO 41 J=2,79
   41 STRING(J)=BLANK
C
C     TRANSFER PHRASE TO STRING
C
      DO 5 I=1,LENGTH
      IND1=IND1+1
      IND2=IND2+1
    5 STRING(IND2) = PHRASE(IND1)
      STRING(1)=PERIOD
      STRING(80) = PERIOD
      PRINT 103
      PRINT 101,(STRING(I),I=1,80)
  101 FORMAT(1H , 80(1H.)/3(2H .,78X,1H./),1H ,80A1/3(2H .,78X,1H./)
     1,1H ,80(1H.))
      GO TO 999
 1000 PRINT 102
  102 FORMAT(1X, 37HBLANK CARD READ IN. EXIT FROM CENTER.)
      CALL EXIT
      END
```

Let us first examine the two errors that mar this otherwise straightforward program. The loop that ends at statement 5 copies the non-blank part of PHRASE into the appropriate part of STRING. Then positions 1 and 80 of the output area, STRING, are overwritten with a PERIOD, regardless of the length of the input. This bodes ill for input strings 79 or 80 characters long. We can avoid the overwrite by putting the two statements that set STRING(1) and STRING(80) before the loop, although it might be better to widen the output to 82 columns instead.

The second bug is more serious. We will leave it as an exercise for the reader to verify that even-length input fields are not centered, but are placed one position too far to the right. When the length is 80, this overwrites STRING(81). This operation is illegal, of course, but few implementations bother to catch it, preferring instead to let you deduce for yourself how some other variable mysteriously changes its value in the middle of a computation.

Rather than trying to patch the errors, let us re-examine the data structure. A moment of study reveals that two arrays, PHRASE and STRING, are used to hold a single piece of data, the original input card. We can eliminate this double representation by creating an array BORDER of 80 blanks with a period on each end, then writing out PHRASE with enough of BORDER on each side to provide the necessary periods and blanks.

```
      INTEGER BLANK, PHRASE(80), BORDER(82), LEFT, LNB, RIGHT, RNB
      DATA BLANK /' '/, BORDER(1) /'.'/, BORDER(82) /'.'/
      DO 10 I = 2, 81
         BORDER(I) = BLANK
   10 CONTINUE
C
   20 READ(5,21) (PHRASE(I), I = 1, 80)
   21    FORMAT(80A1)
C FIND LNB=LEFTMOST NON-BLANK, RNB=RIGHTMOST
      LNB = 0
      DO 30 I = 1, 80
         IF (PHRASE(I) .NE. BLANK) RNB = I
         IF (PHRASE(I) .NE. BLANK .AND. LNB .EQ. 0) LNB = I
   30 CONTINUE
      IF (LNB .EQ. 0) GOTO 90
      LEFT = 1 + (80-(RNB-LNB+1))/2
      RIGHT = 82 - (80-(RNB-LNB+1)+1)/2
      WRITE(6,41) (BORDER(I), I=1,LEFT), (PHRASE(I), I=LNB,RNB),
     $              (BORDER(I), I=RIGHT,82)
   41    FORMAT(1X, 82('.'), /,
     $          3(1X, '.', 80X, '.', /),
     $             1X, 82A1, /,
     $          3(1X, '.', 80X, '.', /),
     $             1X, 82('.') )
      GOTO 20
   90 WRITE(6,91)
   91    FORMAT(1X, 'BLANK CARD READ IN. EXIT FROM CENTER.')
      STOP
      END
```

The actual centering part is now smaller by a factor of three, and that much simpler. As a fringe benefit, it is correct. (This problem is easier in PL/I because variables are permitted in FORMAT statements and because loops can be done zero times. Try it.)

Choosing a better data structure is often an art, which we cannot teach. Often you must write a preliminary draft of the code before you can determine what changes in the data structure will help simplify control. The place to begin such improvements is by asking, "How can I organize the data so the computation becomes as easy as possible?"

Choose a data representation
that makes the program simple.

Excessive use of labels (statement numbers) and GOTO's is often the hallmark of undisciplined design, a sign that a program is out of control. Tracing the flow can be next to impossible if there are too many potential paths from one point to another. Even when such code is correct, it is hard to understand and thus even harder to modify. Consider this program for converting a year and day of the year into the month and day of the month:

```
DATES:    PROC OPTIONS (MAIN);
READ:     GET DATA (IYEAR, IDATE);
          IF IDATE < 1 | IDATE > 366 | IYEAR < 0 THEN RETURN;
          IF IDATE <= 31 THEN GO TO JAN;
          L = 1;
          I = IYEAR/400; IF I = IYEAR/400 THEN GO TO LEAP;
          I = IYEAR/100; IF I = IYEAR/100 THEN GO TO NOLEAP;
          I = IYEAR/4; IF I = IYEAR/4 THEN GO TO LEAP;
NOLEAP:   L = 0;
          IF IDATE > 365 THEN RETURN;
 LEAP:    IF IDATE > 181 + L THEN GO TO G181;
          IF IDATE > 90 + L THEN GO TO G90;
          IF IDATE > 59 + L THEN GO TO G59;
          MONTH = 2; IDAY = IDATE - 31; GO TO OUT;
 G59:     MONTH = 3; IDAY = IDATE - (59 + L); GO TO OUT;
 G90:     IF IDATE > 120 + L THEN GO TO G120;
          MONTH = 4; IDAY = IDATE - (90 + L); GO TO OUT;
 G120:    IF IDATE > 151 + L THEN GO TO G151;
          MONTH = 5; IDAY = IDATE - (120 + L); GO TO OUT;
 G151:    MONTH = 6; IDAY = IDATE - (151 + L); GO TO OUT;
 G181:    IF IDATE > 273 + L THEN GO TO G273;
          IF IDATE > 243 + L THEN GO TO G243;
          IF IDATE > 212 + L THEN GO TO G212;
          MONTH = 7; IDAY = IDATE - (181 + L); GO TO OUT;
 G212:    MONTH = 8; IDAY = IDATE - (212 + L); GO TO OUT;
 G243:    MONTH = 9; IDAY = IDATE - (243 + L); GO TO OUT;
 G273:    IF IDATE > 334 + L THEN GO TO G334;
          IF IDATE > 304 + L THEN GO TO G304;
          MONTH = 10; IDAY = IDATE - (273 + L); GO TO OUT;
 G304:    MONTH = 11; IDAY = IDATE - (304 + L); GO TO OUT;
 G334:    MONTH = 12; IDAY = IDATE - (334 + L);
OUT:      PUT DATA (MONTH,IDAY,IYEAR) SKIP;
          GO TO READ;
 JAN:     MONTH=1; IDAY=IDATE; GO TO OUT;
          END DATES;
```

We have nothing to say about the "structure" of this program; the code speaks for itself. There is one curious usage that bears explaining, however, in the leap year determination. Three lines have the form

```
I = IYEAR/n; IF I = IYEAR/n THEN GO TO label;
```

It would seem that the GOTO is always obeyed, since I surely equals that which was just assigned to it. But in PL/I this is not necessarily so. In the assignment any fractional part is discarded, but in the comparison it is retained. The code thus tests whether IYEAR is divisible by n, and branches if it is. Try to explain that to a novice programmer! Such unobvious code should surely be replaced by

```
IF MOD(IYEAR,n) = 0 THEN GOTO label;
```

This still may not be obvious to a rank beginner, but it is unambiguous and easily learned.

Calendar computations are notoriously complex, but the approach shown above makes them seem even worse. The rococo structure of the calendar is intimately intertwined with the control flow in an attempt to arrive at the proper answer with a minimum number of tests.

Clarity is certainly not worth sacrificing just to save three tests per access (on the average) — the irregularities must be brought under control. In the next chapter we will discuss using subroutines to achieve regularity: the procedure body shows what is common to each invocation, and the differences are concisely summarized in the parameter list for each call. In a similar way, the irregularities in a computation can often be captured in well-chosen data structures. All of the information about how many days precede the first of each month can be put in a table instead of being strung throughout the code. Then a more organized approach is possible. Accordingly, in the first edition of this book, we wrote

```
DATES: PROCEDURE OPTIONS (MAIN);
   DECLARE NDAYS(0:1,0:12) INITIAL(
      0,31,59,90,120,151,181,212,243,273,304,334,365,   /* NON-LEAP */
      0,31,60,91,121,152,182,213,244,274,305,335,366); /* LEAP */

DO WHILE('1'B);
   GET LIST (IYEAR, IDATE) COPY;

   IF MOD(IYEAR,400)=0 |
      (MOD(IYEAR,100)¬=0 & MOD(IYEAR,4)=0)
         THEN LEAP = 1;
         ELSE LEAP = 0;

   IF IYEAR<1753 | IYEAR>3999 | IDATE<=0 | IDATE>NDAYS(LEAP,12)
      THEN PUT SKIP LIST('BAD YEAR, DATE -', IYEAR, IDATE);

   ELSE DO;
      DO MO = 1 TO 12 WHILE (IDATE>NDAYS(LEAP,MO));
      END;

      PUT SKIP LIST(MO, IDATE-NDAYS(LEAP,MO-1), IYEAR);
   END;
END;
END DATES;
```

Even though this code is a single procedure, internally it decomposes into several almost independent pieces. A date is input, LEAP is computed, the date is validated (with excessive zeal), the conversion is made and the result is printed. Each of these pieces could be picked up as a unit and planted as needed in some other environment with a good chance of working unaltered, because there are no unnecessary labels or other cross references between pieces. The control flow structures we have described tend to split programs into *computational units* like these and thus lead to internal modularity.

Yet we can still improve the program, by improving its data structure. A cumulative table of days must be calculated by someone and checked by someone else. Since few people are familiar with the number of days up to the end of a particular month, neither writing nor checking is easy. But if instead we use a table of days per month, we can let the computer count them for us. ("Let the machine do the dirty work.")

```
DATES: PROCEDURE OPTIONS (MAIN);
   DECLARE NDAYS(0:1, 1:12) FIXED BINARY INITIAL(
      31,28,31,30,31,30,31,31,30,31,30,31,    /* NON-LEAP */
      31,29,31,30,31,30,31,31,30,31,30,31);   /* LEAP */
   DECLARE (YEAR, DATE, LEAP, MONTH) FIXED BINARY;
   DECLARE TRUE BIT(1) INITIAL ('1'B);

   DO WHILE (TRUE);
      GET LIST (YEAR, DATE) COPY;

      IF MOD(YEAR,400)=0 | (MOD(YEAR,100)¬=0 & MOD(YEAR,4)=0) THEN
         LEAP = 1;
      ELSE
         LEAP = 0;

      IF YEAR<1753 | YEAR>3999 | DATE<=0 | DATE>365+LEAP THEN
         PUT SKIP LIST('BAD YEAR, DATE -', YEAR, DATE);
      ELSE DO;
         DO MONTH = 1 TO 12 WHILE (DATE > NDAYS(LEAP, MONTH));
            DATE = DATE - NDAYS(LEAP, MONTH);
         END;
         PUT SKIP LIST(MONTH, DATE, YEAR);
      END;
   END;
END DATES;
```

Most people know the lengths of the different months ("Thirty days hath September ..."), so the table in this version can be more quickly checked for accuracy. The program may take a bit more time counting the number of days every time it is called, but it is more likely to get the right answer than you are, and even if the program is used a lot, I/O conversions are sure to use more time than the actual computation of the date. The double computation of NDAYS(LEAP,MONTH) falls into the same category. Write it clearly so it works; then check later whether it's worth your while to rewrite parts of it.

A second, more general, lesson to be drawn from these variations is that no program is ever perfect; there is always room for improvement. Of course, it is foolish to polish a program beyond the point of diminishing returns, but most programmers do too little revision; they are satisfied too early.

Don't stop with your first draft.

We have presented a handful of tools for organizing the control flow and data structures of computer programs. We have also shown what can happen if not enough care is taken in these tasks. This is not to say that these are the only control constructs that lead to intelligible programs. Nor can we guarantee that using just these structures will yield a readable program. But it helps.

The specific points of this chapter are:

(1) Write your program first in a made-up high-level language that you like, where you can see and debug your algorithm. When it is correct and well done, translate it into whatever language you have a compiler for.

(2) The control-flow constructions in your pseudo language should include:

The ability to group statements, as in PL/I's DO-END or BEGIN-END.

IF-ELSE, where the ELSE part is optional.

CASE, which is a multi-way decision. In PL/I it can be written with a series of ELSE-IF's. In Fortran, the computed GOTO can sometimes serve.

DO-WHILE, which repeats a set of statements zero or more times while some condition is true. Note that the range of a Fortran DO is generally executed at least once, so the DO statement must be preceded by an IF and GOTO whenever a zero or negative repeat count might occur.

Subroutines and functions, to break your code into small, separate, manageable pieces.

Your translation should be based on these constructions. GOTO's and labels are suspect; use them sparingly. Any GOTO's and labels in the final product should reflect these constructions only.

(3) Plan your data structures with the same care that you use for the control flow. Try to find a data representation that leads to a simpler program.

POINTS TO PONDER

3.1   Rewrite procedure DATES, using just one array of cumulative days instead of a separate array for leap years:

```
DECLARE NDAYS(0:12)
        INITIAL  (0,31,59,90,120,151,181,212,243,273,304,334,365);
```

Rewrite it using one non-cumulative table of days:

```
DECLARE NDAYS(0:12)
        INITIAL  (0,31,28,31,30,31,30,31,31,30,31,30,31);
```

How do these approaches compare with the ones we showed?

3.2   Revise the following program, after determining what it does.

```
IF X = Y & X = Z & X = W THEN IF X = 0 THEN GO TO DONE;
                              ELSE L1: DO;
                                    SUM = 4*X;
                                    PUT SKIP DATA(SUM);
                                    END L1;
ELSE IF X <= Y THEN
         IF X <= Z THEN
           IF X <= W THEN
             IF Y <= Z THEN
               IF Y <= W THEN
                 IF Z <= W THEN PUT SKIP DATA(X,Y,Z,W);
                 ELSE PUT SKIP DATA(X,Y,W,Z);
               ELSE PUT SKIP DATA(X,W,Y,Z);
             ELSE IF W < Z THEN PUT SKIP DATA(X,W,Z,Y);
                  ELSE IF Y <= W THEN PUT SKIP DATA(X,Z,Y,W);
                       ELSE PUT SKIP DATA(X,Z,W,Y);
           ELSE IF Y <= Z THEN PUT SKIP DATA(W,X,Y,Z);
                ELSE PUT SKIP DATA(W,X,Z,Y);
         ELSE IF W < Z THEN PUT SKIP DATA(W,Z,X,Y);
              ELSE IF W < X THEN PUT SKIP DATA(Z,W,X,Y);
                   ELSE IF  W < Y THEN PUT SKIP DATA(Z,X,W,Y);
                        ELSE PUT SKIP DATA(Z,X,Y,W);
     ELSE IF Y <= Z THEN
           IF Y <= W THEN
             IF X <= Z THEN
               IF X <= W THEN
                 IF Z <= W THEN PUT SKIP DATA(Y,X,Z,W);
                 ELSE PUT SKIP DATA(Y,X,W,Z);
               ELSE PUT SKIP DATA(Y,W,X,Z);
             ELSE IF W < Z THEN PUT SKIP DATA(Y,W,Z,X);
                  ELSE IF X <= W THEN PUT SKIP DATA(Y,Z,X,W);
                       ELSE PUT SKIP DATA(Y,Z,W,X);
           ELSE IF X <= Z THEN PUT SKIP DATA(W,Y,X,Z);
                ELSE PUT SKIP DATA(W,Y,Z,X);
         ELSE IF W < Z THEN PUT SKIP DATA(W,Z,Y,X);
              ELSE IF W < Y THEN PUT SKIP DATA(Z,W,Y,X);
                   ELSE IF W < X THEN PUT SKIP DATA(Z,Y,W,X);
                        ELSE PUT SKIP DATA(Z,Y,X,W);
```

3.3   Rewrite the following Fortran function, attempting to make better use of the regularity of the situation.

```
      FUNCTION KTOSS(KRAND)
C
C THIS FUNCTION GENERATES THE OUTCOME OF A RANDOM TOSS OF TWO DICE
C
      KTOSS=0
      DO 6 I=1,2
      X=XRAND(KRAND)
      IF (X.GT.0.1666667) GO TO 1
      KTOSS=KTOSS+1
      GO TO 6
    1 IF (X.GT.0.3333333) GO TO 2
      KTOSS=KTOSS+2
      GO TO 6
    2 IF (X.GT.0.5) GO TO 3
      KTOSS=KTOSS+3
      GO TO 6
    3 IF (X.GT.0.6666667) GO TO 4
      KTOSS=KTOSS+4
      GO TO 6
    4 IF (X.GT.0.8333333) GO TO 5
      KTOSS=KTOSS+5
      GO TO 6
    5 KTOSS=KTOSS+6
    6 CONTINUE
      RETURN
      END
```

3.4   The following program prints the basic grid for a plotting package. Improve its data structure to improve the plotting accuracy and use the DO loop better.

```
      SUBROUTINE GRAPH1 (PLOT)
      LOGICAL*1 PLOT(50,100)
      LOGICAL*1 BLANK/' '/,DOT/'.'/,A/'A'/,B/'B'/,C/'C'/
      DO 200 L4=1,50
      DO 200 L2=1,100
  200 PLOT(L4,L2)=BLANK
      DO 210 L2=1,100
  210 PLOT(1,L2)=DOT
      DO 211 L2=1,100
  211 PLOT(10,L2)=DOT
      DO 212 L2=1,100
  212 PLOT(20,L2)=DOT
      DO 213 L2=1,100
  213 PLOT(30,L2)=DOT
      DO 214 L2=1,100
  214 PLOT(40,L2)=DOT
      DO 215 L2=1,100
  215 PLOT(50,L2)=DOT
      DO 220 L4=1,50
  220 PLOT(L4,1)=DOT
      DO 221 L4=1,50
  221 PLOT(L4,20)=DOT
      DO 222 L4=1,50
  222 PLOT(L4,40)=DOT
      DO 223 L4=1,50
  223 PLOT(L4,60)=DOT
      DO 224 L4=1,50
  224 PLOT(L4,80)=DOT
      DO 225 L4=1,50
  225 PLOT(L4,100)=DOT
      RETURN
      END
```

3.5   Modify the following program, first by making it into a CASE statement, then by using a different data structure and a loop. Which version is clearer?

```
          TAXPAY=PAY-14.5*NO_EXEMP;
          IF TAXPAY<11.01
              THEN DO;
                          TAX=0;
                          GO TO OUT;
                  END;
          IF TAXPAY<35.01
              THEN DO;
                          TAX=.14*(TAXPAY-11);
                          GO TO OUT;
                  END;
          IF TAXPAY<73.01
              THEN DO;
                          TAX=3.36+.18*(TAXPAY-35);
                          GO TO OUT;
                  END;
          IF TAXPAY<202.01
              THEN DO;
                          TAX=10.20+.21*(TAXPAY-73);
                          GO TO OUT;
                  END;
          IF TAXPAY<231.01
              THEN DO;
                          TAX=37.29+.23*(TAXPAY-202);
                          GO TO OUT;
                  END;
          IF TAXPAY<269.01
              THEN DO;
                          TAX=43.96+.27*(TAXPAY-231);
                          GO TO OUT;
                  END;
          IF TAXPAY<333.01
              THEN DO;
                          TAX=54.22+.31*(TAXPAY-269);
                          GO TO OUT;
                  END;
                          TAX=74.06+.35*(TAXPAY-333);
      OUT:
          ...
```

CHAPTER 4: **PROGRAM STRUCTURE**

Most programs are too big to be comprehended as a single chunk. They must be divided into smaller pieces that can be conquered separately. That is the only way to write them reliably; it is the only way to read and understand them.

Subroutines, functions, and procedures are the "modules," or building blocks, of large programs. In many languages, they can be compiled separately and, if properly designed, maintained nearly independently of each other. Well designed building blocks are often usable in other applications, contributing to a library of labor-saving routines.

When a program is not broken up into small enough pieces, the larger modules often fail to deliver on these promises. They try to do too much, or too many different things, and hence are difficult to maintain and are too specialized for general use.

Consider the following subroutine, which generates simple moves (no jumps) for a checker-playing program. The routine tries to make up to four moves: forward right and left, backward right and left. If the move is off the board or to an occupied square, it is disallowed. White men may only move forward and black men may only move backward. Kings may move either way.

```
        SUBROUTINE SEARCH (BOARD,I,J,MOVROW,MOVCOL,L)
        DIMENSION BOARD(8,8),MOVROW(4),MOVCOL(4)
        INTEGER BOARD
C       ASSUME THE CHECKERS ARE CODED AS FOLLOWS:
C           1-WHITE MAN
C               2-WHITE KING
C                   3-BLACK MAN
C                       4-BLACK KING
C       BOARD IS THE ARRAY REPRESENTING THE
C       CHECKER BOARD WITH 0'S IN POSITIONS WITH
C       NO MEN, I AND J ARE THE COORDINATES OF
C       THE MAN WHOSE MOVES ARE BEING SEARCHED
C       FOR, MOVROW AND MOVCOL ARE ARRAYS WHICH
C       ARE TO CONTAIN THE ROW AND COLUMN COORDINATES
C       OF POSSIBLE MOVES AND L COUNTS THE NUMBER OF
C       POSSIBLE MOVES ***
C       IF(BOARD(I,J) IS ZERO, ERROR HAS BEEN MADE
        IF(BOARD(I,J).EQ.0) STOP
        L=0
        K=BOARD(I,J)
C       ASSUME WHITE MEN START IN ROWS ONE
C       TO THREE, BLACK MEN IN ROWS SIX TO EIGHT.....
        GO TO (4,4,6,4),K
C       ENTRY FOR ALL EXCEPT BLACK MAN
C       FORWARD RIGHT
C       TEST IF MOVE IS ON BOARD
      4 IF(I.EQ.8) GO TO 8
        IF(J.EQ.8) GO TO 2
        IF(BOARD(I+1,J+1).NE.0) GO TO 2
        L=L+1
        MOVROW(L)=I+1
        MOVCOL(L)=J+1
C       FORWARD LEFT
      2 IF(J.EQ.1) GO TO 8
        IF(BOARD(I+1,J-1).NE.0) GO TO 8
        L=L+1
        MOVROW(L)=I+1
        MOVCOL(L)=J-1
C       EXIT TEST FOR WHITE MAN
      8 IF(K.EQ.1) RETURN
C       BACKWARD RIGHT
      6 IF(I.EQ.1) RETURN
        IF(J.EQ.8) GO TO 10
        IF(BOARD(I-1,J+1).NE.0) GO TO 10
        L=L+1
        MOVROW(L)=I-1
        MOVCOL(L)=J+1
C       BACKWARD LEFT
     10 IF(J.EQ.1) RETURN
        IF(BOARD(I-1,J-1).NE.0) RETURN
        L=L+1
        MOVROW(L)=I-1
        MOVCOL(L)=J-1
        RETURN
        END
```

Again, the repeated tests, with no obvious pattern, should alert us to a possible structural weakness. Some combination of statements ought surely to be isolated as a second subroutine, to modularize the code. If we do not fret over making a few "unnecessary" tests, we can unsnarl the tangle of branches with a general "test and store" subroutine, which decides whether one specified direction represents a legal move, and saves it. All that is left then is the constraint on what men may make certain moves, which can be simply encoded:

```
      SUBROUTINE SEARCH(BOARD, I, J, ROW, COL, L)
      INTEGER BOARD(8,8), ROW(4), COL(4)
C             BOARD(I,J)=0 => EMPTY SQUARE
C                        1 => WHITE MAN, 2 => WHITE KING
C                        3 => BLACK MAN, 4 => BLACK KING
C             I INCREASES FORWARD, J INCREASES RIGHT
C             L COUNTS THE MOVES STORED IN ROW,COL
      IF (I.LT.1 .OR. I.GT.8 .OR. J.LT.1 .OR. J.GT.8)
     $    CALL ERROR(9, 'OFF BOARD')
      K = BOARD(I,J)
      IF (K.LT.1 .OR. K.GT.4) CALL ERROR(20, 'ILLEGAL MAN ON BOARD')
      L = 0
      IF (K .NE. 3) CALL STORE(BOARD, I+1, J+1, ROW, COL, L)
      IF (K .NE. 3) CALL STORE(BOARD, I+1, J-1, ROW, COL, L)
      IF (K .NE. 1) CALL STORE(BOARD, I-1, J+1, ROW, COL, L)
      IF (K .NE. 1) CALL STORE(BOARD, I-1, J-1, ROW, COL, L)
      RETURN
      END

      SUBROUTINE STORE(BOARD, IC, JC, ROW, COL, L)
      INTEGER BOARD(8,8), ROW(4), COL(4)
      IF (IC.LT.1 .OR. IC.GT.8 .OR. JC.LT.1 .OR. JC.GT.8) RETURN
      IF (BOARD(IC,JC) .NE. 0) RETURN
      L = L+1
      ROW(L) = IC
      COL(L) = JC
      RETURN
      END
```

Separating code into appropriate modules is an important aspect of writing a program. As we can see here, the subroutine call permits us to summarize the *irregularities* in the argument list, where we can see quickly what is going on. The subroutine itself summarizes the *regularities* of the code, so repeated patterns need not be used. An added advantage of this version is that including complexities like jumps later on will be rather easy. "Optimizing" too early in the life of a program can kill its chances for growth.

We have included calls to an unspecified error-printing routine, to simplify the handling of illegal inputs. Such a subroutine can overcome the inertia normally felt when it comes time to check for possible errors. Some people feel that the calls to ERROR should be inserted "until the program is debugged," then removed. Leave them in indefinitely — the insurance is cheap.

Modularize.   Use subroutines.

Breaking a program into arbitrary pieces is not sufficient, however. The integration program at the end of Chapter 2 actually benefited by *eliminating* a separate module. This was because there were too many shared assumptions between the calling and called routines. Since it was not possible to ignore either module while studying the other, the separation of operations into two groups simply made more work, forcing the reader to skip back and forth.

Here is the subprocedure OUT once again:

```
OUT: PROCEDURE;
        AREA = AREA + LMTS;
     PUT SKIP EDIT  (MSSG3,K,AREA)  (X(2),A(16),F(2),X(6),
            F(9,6));
      AREA = 0;
      RETURN;
     END;
```

To do its assigned task, OUT must be privy to the values of AREA, LMTS, MSSG3, and K. Moreover it relies on the calling routine to perform part of the AREA calculation; the calling routine in turn depends on OUT to reinitialize AREA to zero.

There is no way one can summarize all these relationships succinctly enough to permit separate maintenance of the two routines — yet that is the essence of modularity. It must be possible to describe the *function* performed by a module in the briefest of terms; and it is necessary to minimize whatever relationships exist with other modules, and display those that remain as explicitly as possible. This is how we obtain the minimum "coupling," and hence maximum independence, between modules.

In the case of OUT, this means that the AREA calculations should be performed completely in the calling routine, and the literal value of MSSG3 written in place of the variable. If we wish to keep this as a separate module, small as it has now become, then the remaining shared data, AREA and K, should be explicitly passed as arguments:

```
OUT: PROCEDURE(K, AREA);    /* PRINT STEP SIZE AND AREA */
     DECLARE K FIXED DECIMAL (2),
          AREA FIXED DECIMAL (8, 6);

     PUT SKIP EDIT ('FOR DELTA X = 1/', K, AREA)
                (X(2), A, F(2), X(6), F(9, 6));
     END;
```

Make the coupling between modules visible.

There are other considerations besides coupling that affect how to modularize a program. The following program computes the median of a set of numbers, and tells whether the number of elements is even or odd.

```
ST14_3: PROCEDURE OPTIONS (MAIN);
  ON ENDFILE (SYSIN) GO TO OD_EV;
  DCL X(100) FIXED (3) INITIAL ((100)0);
  DCL HALF FIXED (4,2) INITIAL (0);
  I = 1;
INLOOP: GET LIST (X(I));
  I = I + 1;
  GO TO INLOOP;
OD_EV: HALF = (I - 1) / 2;
  IF HALF = TRUNC(HALF) THEN DO;
    A = X(HALF);
    B = X(HALF + 1);
    CALL EV_ARY (A,B);
    END;
  ELSE DO;
    A = X(TRUNC(HALF) + 1);
    CALL OD_ARY (A);
    END;
END;

EV_ARY: PROCEDURE (R,S);
  DCL MEDIAN FIXED (5, 2) INITIAL (0);
  MEDIAN = (R + S) / 2;
  PUT SKIP LIST ('ARRAY HAS EVEN NUMBER OF ENTRIES');
  PUT SKIP DATA (MEDIAN);
  END EV_ARY;

OD_ARY: PROCEDURE (R);
  DCL MEDIAN FIXED (5, 2) INITIAL (0);
  MEDIAN = R;
  PUT SKIP LIST ('ARRAY HAS ODD  NUMBER OF ENTRIES');
  PUT SKIP DATA (MEDIAN);
  END OD_ARY;
```

If you find the code a bit hard to understand, it's probably because it's hard to figure out what HALF does. HALF has an inappropriate data type — although it's actually an integer because it represents an array index, it's typed FIXED DECIMAL with two decimal places. The built-in function TRUNC is used to truncate any fractional part, in a strange test for divisibility.

But the biggest problem lies in the choice of modules used to express the solution. EV_ARY is called when there are an even number of X's, so two adjacent elements are needed to compute the median, which is then printed. OD_ARY is similar, but different — only one element is needed to determine the median, so only that one is passed as an argument.

Two such similar functions ought surely be combined into one more generally useful routine. It seems silly to have a function that can compute the median only of arrays with an even number of elements; it is even sillier to require the calling routine to perform half the calculation (determining which elements are needed to compute the median), then decide which of two specialized functions should finish the job. A true MEDIAN function, on the other hand, is likely to be usable in a number of contexts. It is also much easier to describe what it does.

But it is not enough just to combine the two functions OD_ARY and EV_ARY, because in addition to not doing enough, each also does *too much*. Why print the result from inside the routine that computes the median? The print operation has nothing to do with the calculation; it merely happens to use the result. A more general function would simply compute the median of an array and return it to the calling program. The resulting value can be used in further calculations, or stored, or printed in a variety of formats, depending on the application. Combining too many functions in one module is a sure way to limit its usefulness, while at the same time making it more complex and harder to maintain.

Each module should do one thing well.

Here is the same program modularized a different way:

```
ST14_3: PROCEDURE OPTIONS (MAIN);
   /* READ A LIST AND PRINT MEDIAN */
   DECLARE (N, X(100)) FIXED DECIMAL (3);

   N = GETLIST(X, 100);
   IF N = 0 THEN
      PUT SKIP LIST ('ARRAY HAS NO ENTRIES');
   ELSE DO;
      IF MOD(N, 2) = 0 THEN
         PUT SKIP LIST ('ARRAY HAS EVEN NUMBER OF ENTRIES');
      ELSE
         PUT SKIP LIST ('ARRAY HAS ODD NUMBER OF ENTRIES');
      PUT SKIP LIST ('MEDIAN IS', MEDIAN(X, N));
   END;

GETLIST: PROCEDURE (X, MAXN) RETURNS (FIXED DECIMAL (3));
   /* READ AT MOST MAXN ITEMS INTO ARRAY X */
   DECLARE (X(*), MAXN, I) FIXED DECIMAL(3);

   ON ENDFILE (SYSIN)
      GOTO DONE;

   DO I = 1 TO MAXN;
      GET LIST (X(I));
   END;
   RETURN (MAXN);
DONE:
   RETURN (I-1);
END;
```

```
MEDIAN: PROCEDURE (X, N) RETURNS (FIXED DECIMAL (5, 2));
   DECLARE (X(*), N) FIXED DECIMAL (3);

   IF N <= 0 THEN
      RETURN(0);
   ELSE IF MOD(N, 2) = 0 THEN
      RETURN((X(N/2) + X(N/2 + 1)) / 2);
   ELSE
      RETURN(X((N+1)/2));
   END;

END;
```

Testing whether N is zero both in the main routine and in MEDIAN may seem like paranoia, but it is actually a small example of defensive programming, a topic we will talk more about in Chapter 6. Someday, someone else will use the median routine, and it would be nice to know that it will do its task sensibly even if the user doesn't take special precautions.

We also chose to isolate the business of reading a list of numbers in a separate procedure because it is a task that occurs in many programs. Not only that, but it involves a messy test for end of file that is expressed in PL/I by an ON-condition and a GOTO. The bulk of the program does not have to know what is involved in detecting the end of input data. In fact, it is much better off *not* knowing exactly what mechanism is used; the input code only adds to the general confusion and may well have to be changed later on.

For all these reasons, it is best to hide the details of reading a list of numbers inside a function that has a simple interface to the outside world. Input/output is almost always messy and subject to change, so we make a point of hiding input and output in separate modules. One good test of the worth of a module, in fact, is how good a job it does of hiding some aspect of the problem from the rest of the code.

Make sure every module hides something.

Program organization, deciding what gets done where, is often given insufficient consideration. This can be true even when the format of input or output data strongly suggests the most convenient order of processing. Failure to heed such suggestions leads to code that is hard to relate to the problem being solved, and hence likely to contain mistakes. Here is part of a program for processing customer accounts:

```
    CTR = 0;
  GO TO OVFLO;
  RDCARD: READ FILE (CARDIN) INTO (CARD);
/*TABLE LOOKUP FOR VALID CUSTOMER NUMBER*/
    LOOP: DO I = 1 TO 20;
      IF CARD.NUM = NUM_TBL(I)
    THEN GO TO NN;
          ELSE;
      END;
    GO TO RDCARD;
    NN: ...

 IF CARD.AMT > 0 THEN GO TO CR_RTN;
          ELSE GO TO DR_RTN;
    CR_RTN: DETAIL.CREDIT = CARD.AMT;
    DETAIL.DEBIT = 0;
      WRITE FILE (PRTFLE) FROM (DETAIL);
            GO TO TST_CTR;
    DR_RTN: DETAIL.DEBIT = CARD.AMT;
    DETAIL.CREDIT = 0;
      WRITE FILE (PRTFLE) FROM (DETAIL);
    TST_CTR: CTR = CTR + 1;
            IF CTR > 45 THEN GO TO OVFLO;
          ELSE GO TO RDCARD;
    OVFLO:
    WRITE FILE (PRTFLE) FROM (HDR);
    WRITE FILE (PRTFLE)  FROM (COL_HDR);
    WRITE FILE (PRTFLE) FROM (LINE);
      CTR = 0;
    GO TO RDCARD;
```

The program evidently intends to produce a report with a header and up to 46 detail lines per page. But what happens if there are zero transactions, or exactly 46, or 92, or any other multiple of 46? Sure enough, the column headings are printed on an extra page, even though there is no data to go under them. The test for end-of-page should happen before line 47 is printed, not after line 46.

The problem is that the structure of the program is only loosely related to the structure of the output report to be generated. It should be no surprise that the two structures don't always agree. What we want to generate can be described as

zero or more pages, each of which has
  a header, and
  one to 46 detail lines

We should be able to use our knowledge of the report format to find our way around in the code; yet the header is generated near the bottom of the program and cards are read for the detail lines near the top. The GOTO at the top of the program is a giveaway that things don't happen naturally at the right places.

A pseudo-code program that more closely resembles the report format is

```
WHILE (there's more input)
  IF (we're at top of page)
    write header
  compute detail information
  write detail line
```

This calls for reading an input record and using the success or failure of that operation to control the loop. Since that is not a simple operation, we make a separate module to isolate that complexity from the code that produces the output report.

The result:

```
CTR = 0;
DO WHILE (GETCARD() = YES);
    IF ¬ANY(NUM_TBL = CARD.NUM) THEN
        PUT SKIP LIST ('BAD CARD', CARD.NUM, CARD.AMT);
    ELSE DO;
        CTR = CTR + 1;
        IF MOD(CTR, 46) = 1 THEN DO;    /* HEADER */
            WRITE FILE (PRTFLE) FROM (HDR);
            WRITE FILE (PRTFLE) FROM (COL_HDR);
            WRITE FILE (PRTFLE) FROM (LINE);
        END;
        IF CARD.AMT > 0 THEN DO;
            DETAIL.CREDIT = CARD.AMT;
            DETAIL.DEBIT = 0;
        END;
        ELSE DO;
            DETAIL.CREDIT = 0;
            DETAIL.DEBIT = CARD.AMT;
        END;
        WRITE FILE (PRTFLE) FROM (DETAIL);
    END;
END;
```

This takes care of producing the report, leaving the problem of input to a separate module:

```
GETCARD: PROCEDURE RETURNS (BIT(1));
    ON ENDFILE (CARDIN)
        GOTO EOF;
    READ FILE (CARDIN) INTO (CARD);
    RETURN (YES);
EOF:
    RETURN (NO);
END;
```

GETCARD merely reads a card each time it is called; it signals end of file when there is no data left.

Let the data structure the program.

Modularity becomes most important when a program starts getting large, so we will devote the rest of this chapter to a single example that is big enough to illustrate several principles of program structure. The following program simulates a mouse trying to find a path through a maze by the simple rule, "Turn right if you can, left if you must." The maze is a Boolean matrix, with ones representing possible paths and zeros the walls. A path consists of a connected series of horizontal and vertical strings of ones that enters the maze somewhere and exits somewhere else. A path may not run along the edge, although its ends may both be on one side. For example, the maze on the left below has a solution as shown on the right.

```
00010        XXX X
11110          X X
01010        X X X
01110        X   X
00000        XXXXX
```

As you read the code, remember that a big program should be a collection of manageable pieces, each of which must obey the rules of good style.

```
EX510:PROCEDURE OPTIONS(MAIN);

/*   FIRST ASSUME MAXIMUM DIMENSIONS FOR THE MAZE  -  HERE 50 X 50   */
  DCL (POINT(2,60),X,Y,(POSITIONX,POSITIONY)(2500)) DEC FIXED(4),
         MAZE(50,50) BIT(1),XMAZE(50,50) CHAR(1) ,
         BRANCH LABEL(LOOKL,LOOKR,LOOKU,LOOKD);
         XMAZE='X';
  GET LIST(N,M);

   GET EDIT(((MAZE(I,J) DO J=1 TO N) DO I=1 TO M))(COLUMN(1),(N)B(1));
   PUT EDIT(((MAZE(I,J) DO J=1 TO N) DO I=1 TO M))(LINE(33-M/2),
          (M) (COLUMN(40-N/2),(N) B(1),SKIP));
     I,MM,NN=1;      II,IN1,IN2=0;

/*  NEXT FIND A PATH THROUGH THE MAZE  -  THIS IS DONE BY SIMULATING
  A MAN KEEPING HIS RIGHT HAND IN CONTACT WITH THE WALL AND FOLLOWING IT  */

   RUNUD:DO K1=NN TO N BY N-1;
         DO K2=IN1+1 TO M;
         IF MAZE(K2,K1)='1'B THEN GO TO TEST1;
   END RUNUD;

   RUNLR:DO K1=MM TO M BY M-1;
         DO K2=IN2 TO N;
         IF MAZE(K1,K2)='1'B THEN GO TO TEST2;
   END RUNLR;

   TEST1:X,NN=K2;          POSITIONX(1)=X;
         Y,IN1=K1;         POSITIONY(1)=Y;
         IF NN=1 THEN GO TO LOOKR;
                     GO TO LOOKL;

   TEST2:Y,MM=K2;          POSITIONY(1)=Y;
         X,IN2=K1;         POSITIONX(1)=X;
         IF MM=1 THEN GO TO LOOKD;
```

```
     LOOKU:IF MAZE(X-1,Y)='1'B THEN DO;
           BRANCH=LOOKR;            X=X-1;
              GO TO SET;
                                 END;

     LOOKL:IF MAZE(X,Y-1)='1'B THEN DO ;
           BRANCH=LOOKU;            Y=Y-1;
              GO TO SET;
                                   END;

     LOOKD:IF MAZE(X+1,Y)='1'B THEN DO;
           BRANCH=LOOKL;            X=X+1;
              GO TO SET;
                                 END;

     LOOKR:IF MAZE(X,Y+1)='1'B THEN DO;
           BRANCH=LOOKD;            Y=Y+1;
              GO TO SET;
                             END;
                             ELSE GO TO LOOKU;

        SET:I=I+1;

        POSITIONX(I)=X;            POSITIONY(I)=Y;

     IF X<N&X>1&Y<M&Y>1 THEN GO TO BRANCH;

     IF X=POSITIONX(1)&Y=POSITIONY(1) THEN DO;
           IF IN2=0 THEN GO TO RUNUD;
                    ELSE GO TO RUNLR;
                          END;

/*  NOW PICK OUT THOSE PARTS OF THE PATH FOLLOWED WHICH WENT IN A LOOP OR
       DEAD ENDED   */

/* NOTE THE TRANSFER STATEMENT WHICH CAUSES A TRANSFER TO WHAT LOOKS
   LIKE THE NEXT STATEMENT  -  ACTUALLY THE COMPILER CREATES A DUMMY STATEMENT
   BETWEEN THESE TWO TO END THE INNER DO LOOP  -  HENCE  THE PROGRAM MUST
   BRANCH AROUND IT   */

   SORT:DO J=I TO 2 BY-1;
       DO K=J-1 TO 1 BY -1;
           IF POSITIONX(K)=POSITIONX(J)&POSITIONY(K)=POSITIONY(J)
                  THEN DO;        II=II+1;       POINT(1,II)=J;
                      POINT(2,II)=K;    J=K+1;     GO TO ENDSORT;
   ENDSORT:END SORT;

/*  FINALLY SET UP THE FINAL MAZE WITH THE PATH FOLLOWED    */

   MERGE:DO KK=1 TO I;
           DO IK=1 TO II;
               IF KK=POINT(2,IK) THEN KK=POINT(1,IK);
           END;

       XMAZE(POSITIONX(KK),POSITIONY(KK))=' ';
   END MERGE;
   PUT PAGE EDIT(((XMAZE(I,J) DO J=1 TO N) DO I=1 TO M))(LINE(33-M/2),
       (M) (COLUMN(40-N/2),(N) A(1),SKIP));

END EX510;
```

The interesting thing about this program is that it successfully ran a test case, despite all the errors we are about to unearth. To debug this code by running test cases alone would clearly take a long time. Just proofreading is hard enough, because the control logic is so curiously distributed. Let us analyze the code by sections.

The DO loops at RUNUD and RUNLR inspect the borders of the maze, looking for an entrance. TEST1 and TEST2 start the mouse going "in" from an opening by transferring control to the appropriate LOOKx test. These implement the right-turn rule described above, either to find a path continuation or to cause the mouse to back out of a dead end. SET stores each point along the path and tests whether the mouse has reached the border again. If the mouse comes out where it went in, this is not a path, so the program goes back to the appropriate RUNxx loop to continue searching the border where it left off. Otherwise it falls through to the SORT and MERGE loops, which determine the path to be printed out.

The RUNxx loops have elaborate control parameters so that they can be resumed. This is not an easy thing to do, so we are not surprised to find that it is done wrong. At TEST1, for instance, we see that NN remembers the index K2; but at RUNUD, NN is associated with the index K1. Sure enough, the lower limits for all four DO loops are stored incorrectly. The program cannot properly resume the border scan.

There are other problems with these DO loops. If the maze has no entry points, or if there is no path through it, control falls through to TEST1 and the program starts looking around outside the array MAZE. (Watch out for DO loops that "never" terminate normally.) By definition, it is not possible to go "in" from a corner, yet each is tried and could give an uninteresting answer — a path that only runs along the edge. In fact, any adjacent ones on the border will be reported as a path. Finally, the two inner loops (on K2) are handled differently even though they perform similar functions. This tips us off that one of them is incorrect. (As a matter of fact both are, but the details are not worth pursuing.)

The four LOOKx tests form one of those repeated patterns we have already encountered several times. Defining the appropriate data structures should permit us to summarize all four tests in one. Then perhaps we could avoid the dubious GOTO BRANCH, which is a PL/I equivalent of Fortran's assigned GOTO and equally obscure. Anything that disguises the flow of control should be avoided.

SORT and MERGE are correctly coded, but not well designed. It seems silly to save all the loops and dead ends encountered until the very end, when they can be readily eliminated along the way. Then it is not necessary to make a list of all the matching points so that loops can be skipped over on output. (POINT should be written as two arrays, by the way, and each should be much larger than 60 elements. POSITIONX and POSITIONY, on the other hand, need be only about two thirds of their current size of 2500.) SORT and MERGE are far more complicated than necessary.

Finally, the sequence

```
                    GO TO ENDSORT;
            ENDSORT:END SORT;
```

is an open invitation to misunderstanding. The fact that a four line comment is needed to explain what is going on should be reason enough to rewrite the code. An even better reason is that the comment is wrong — *two* dummy statements are created to end *two* DO groups. How much easier and clearer it is to write

```
            GOTO ENDSORT;
        END;
    END;
ENDSORT: END SORT;
```

There are too many other errors to discuss in detail. An isolated border cell with value `'1'B` will cause grief, as will a non-square maze. Even for a maze as trivial as

```
000
111
000
```

the correct path is never found; when we ran it, after an indeterminate amount of poking around outside the maze the program reported that the middle cell on the left border forms a "path." When subscript range checking is turned on, the program aborts.

It is an enlightening exercise to patch the maze program, providing just enough corrections to permit it to handle reasonable inputs. But patching only serves to emphasize the shortcomings of this organization. After a brief attempt, most readers will agree that the best cure is not revision but a total rewrite.

Don't patch bad code — rewrite it.

The maze program is big enough that it is well worth while planning its structure carefully. One of the better ways of doing this is what is often called "top-down design." In a top-down design, we start with a very general pseudo-code statement of the program like

```
solve mazes
```

and then elaborate this statement in stages, filling in details until we ultimately reach executable code. Not only does this help to keep the structure fairly well organized, and avoid getting bogged down in coding too early, but it also means that we can back up and alter bad decisions without losing too much investment.

How do we "solve mazes"? The loop

```
WHILE (there's a maze)
    solve it
```

breaks the job into two clean pieces — checking whether a maze exists, and processing it. Usually the easiest way to find out whether there is a maze is to try to read it in, using a separate input procedure. This is a convenient organization, as we shall see here and again in Chapter 5.

Refining further,

```
WHILE (READMAZE() = YES)
    IF (there's a path)
        print it
    ELSE
        print 'no path'
```

This specifies the input function interface more clearly, and shows where the printing is done. It also implies that we need a procedure that tests whether there is a path, which is obviously the hard part. In fact, since this is a big job, it might be desirable to write READMAZE completely and test it before we go on with path-finding.

We will represent the maze by a bit array with one value for a wall and the other for a non-wall, just as in the original. Then READMAZE is the following:

```
READMAZE: PROCEDURE RETURNS (BIT(1));

      ON ENDFILE(SYSIN)
         GOTO EOF;
      GET LIST (M, N);
      IF M < 2 | M > 50 | N < 2 | N > 50 THEN DO;
         PUT SKIP LIST (M, N, 'BAD DIMENSIONS');
         RETURN(NO);
      END;
      GET EDIT (((MAZE(I,J) DO J = 1 TO N) DO I = 1 TO M))
         (COLUMN(1), (N)B(1));
      PUT PAGE EDIT (((MAZE(I,J) DO J = 1 TO N) DO I = 1 TO M))
         (COLUMN(1), (N)B(1));
      RETURN(YES);
   EOF:
      RETURN(NO);
   END READMAZE;
```

Now we can write an abbreviated main routine that calls only READMAZE, and test it before any more code is added to confuse the logic.

With READMAZE out of the way, we can continue with the procedure FINDPATH, which searches a maze for a path. Basically, FINDPATH must probe at the maze from each edge. If it ever finds a path, it returns YES; otherwise it returns NO.

```
   FINDPATH()
      IF (path from left side)
         return(YES)
      ELSE IF (path from right side)
         return(YES)
      ELSE IF (path from top)
         return(YES)
      ELSE IF (path from bottom)
         return(YES)
      ELSE
         return(NO)
```

Suppose we put the details of how to look for a path from a particular edge into a separate procedure called TRY, where we can use arguments to indicate what edge and direction is of interest in a particular call.

TRY looks at the cell under consideration. If this is a wall, then there can be no path, and TRY can return NO immediately. If the cell is not a wall, TRY can search from the cell in each direction in turn.

```
TRY()
    IF (this cell is a wall)
        return(NO)
    ELSE IF (path from this cell in any direction)
        return(YES)
    ELSE
        return(NO);
```

We have now come to something that actually looks difficult — how can we find out whether there is a path from a point to the edge in a particular direction?

The maze can get pretty big, and neither a mouse nor a computer can consider much of it at any one time. Whatever strategy mouse or machine adopts should be a "local" one, in the sense that only a small neighborhood of cells is ever considered at once and that the same strategy is used regardless of where the neighborhood lies in the maze.

A powerful tool for reducing apparent complexity is recursion. In a recursive procedure, the method of solution is defined in terms of itself. That is, each part of the routine handles only a small piece of the strategy, then calls the other parts of the routine as needed to handle the rest. The trick is to reduce each hard case to one that is handled simply elsewhere.

The mouse in a maze problem is a natural for recursion. Imagine that the mouse is sitting somewhere in the middle of the maze wondering if there if a path from where he is. If he is a clever mouse, he will realize that there is a path from where he is to the border if

(1) there is an adjacent accessible cell that he hasn't already looked at, and

(2) there is a path from that cell.

Answering (1) is trivial. And the answer to (2) can be determined in exactly the same way as the original question, except that the mouse is presumably one step nearer to a solution. Thus the solution process is defined in terms of itself: recursion.

Although defining the solution recursively sounds like an infinite loop, it does terminate. Searching stops when the mouse finds a path, or when he has checked out all possibilities without success.

Let us see how recursion applies to path-finding. Suppose we define a recursive function $TRY(i1,j1,i2,j2)$ which returns YES if there is a path from the point $(i1,j1)$ through adjacent point $(i2,j2)$ that leads to the edge. If there is no path, TRY returns NO. How does it work?

If $(i1,j1)$ is a wall, there is certainly no path. If we've previously investigated $(i2,j2)$ without success or if it's a wall, there is no path. If $(i2,j2)$ is an edge cell, there is a path. Otherwise, we simply put $(i1,j1)$ on the path tentatively, step over to $(i2,j2)$ (making it the current $(i1,j1)$), then look in the four directions from there. If there's a path from one of them, there's a path from $(i1,j1)$, otherwise there isn't.

This is actually clearer in pseudo-code:

```
TRY(i1,j1,i2,j2)    is there a path from i1,j1 using i2,j2?
  IF (maze(i1,j1) is a wall)
     return(NO)
  IF (maze(i2,j2) is a wall)
     return(NO)
  IF (we've been to i2,j2 before)
     return(NO)
  remember that we've been to i1,j1
  put i1,j1 on the path tentatively
  IF (i2,j2 is at edge of maze)
     put i2,j2 on path too
     return(YES)
  ELSE IF (path from up cell adjacent to i2,j2)
     return(YES)
  ELSE IF (path from right cell adjacent to i2,j2)
     return(YES)
  ELSE IF (path from down cell adjacent to i2,j2)
     return(YES)
  ELSE IF (path from left cell adjacent to i2,j2)
     return(YES)
  ELSE
     take i1,j1 off the path
     return(NO)
```

Each test of the form

```
  ELSE IF (path from ... cell adjacent to i2,j2)
```

is performed by calling TRY. In this way, TRY handles only a small part of the problem directly, then calls itself recursively when necessary to handle the rest.

Finally, we must consider the question of data representation. We have to record things like whether we've been to a cell before, and also what the actual path is. One simple possibility is to record in an array STATE whether we've been to a cell before or not. The array STATE contains two states, "used" (meaning we've looked at this square before), and "free" (meaning we haven't). We could also use STATE to record the path as it is found, or (as we choose here), use two linear arrays IPATH and JPATH to record the coordinates of the path as it is found. This latter organization takes a bit more code, but is substantially faster, since we never follow a blind alley more than once.

Putting all of these pieces together makes a large program, but no larger than the original, and markedly easier to follow.

```
MOUSE: PROCEDURE OPTIONS (MAIN);
    /* MOUSE IN A MAZE */
    /* SEARCHES PERIPHERY OF M X N MATRIX FOR AN ENTRY POINT */
    /* FIRST PATH WITH EXIT DIFFERENT FROM ENTRANCE IS ACCEPTED */

    DECLARE (YES INITIAL('1'B), NO INITIAL('0'B)) BIT(1);
    DECLARE MAZE(50,50) BIT(1);
    DECLARE WALL BIT(1) INITIAL('0'B);
    DECLARE STATE(50,50) CHARACTER(1);
    DECLARE USED CHARACTER(1) INITIAL('U');
    DECLARE FREE CHARACTER(1) INITIAL('F');
    DECLARE (PATHPTR, IPATH(2000), JPATH(2000)) FIXED BINARY;
    DECLARE (M, N) FIXED BINARY;

    DO WHILE (READMAZE() = YES);
        IF FINDPATH() = YES THEN
            CALL PRINTPATH;
        ELSE
            PUT SKIP(2) LIST ('NO PATH');
    END;

READMAZE: PROCEDURE RETURNS (BIT(1));
    ON ENDFILE(SYSIN)
        GOTO EOF;
    GET LIST (M, N);
    IF M < 2 | M > 50 | N < 2 | N > 50 THEN DO;
        PUT SKIP LIST (M, N, 'BAD DIMENSIONS');
        RETURN(NO);
    END;
    GET EDIT (((MAZE(I,J) DO J = 1 TO N) DO I = 1 TO M))
        (COLUMN(1), (N)B(1));
    PUT PAGE EDIT (((MAZE(I,J) DO J = 1 TO N) DO I = 1 TO M))
        (COLUMN(1), (N)B(1));
    RETURN(YES);
EOF:
    RETURN(NO);
END READMAZE;

FINDPATH: PROCEDURE RETURNS (BIT(1));
    STATE(*, *) = FREE;
    PATHPTR = 0;
    DO I = 2 TO M-1;
        IF TRY(I, 1, I, 2) THEN    /* LEFT SIDE */
            RETURN(YES);
        IF TRY(I, N, I, N-1) THEN   /* RIGHT SIDE */
            RETURN(YES);
    END;
    DO J = 2 TO N-1;
        IF TRY(1, J, 2, J) THEN    /* TOP */
            RETURN(YES);
        IF TRY(M, J, M-1, J) THEN   /* BOTTOM */
            RETURN(YES);
    END;
    RETURN(NO);
END FINDPATH;
```

```
TRY: PROCEDURE(I1, J1, I2, J2) RECURSIVE RETURNS (BIT(1));
   DECLARE (I1, J1, I2, J2) FIXED BINARY;

   IF MAZE(I1, J1) = WALL THEN
      RETURN(NO);
   IF MAZE(I2, J2) = WALL | STATE(I2, J2) = USED THEN
      RETURN(NO);
   STATE(I1, J1) = USED;
   PATHPTR = PATHPTR + 1;
   IPATH(PATHPTR) = I1;
   JPATH(PATHPTR) = J1;
   IF I2 = 1 | I2 = M | J2 = 1 | J2 = N THEN DO;
      STATE(I2, J2) = USED;
      PATHPTR = PATHPTR + 1;
      IPATH(PATHPTR) = I2;
      JPATH(PATHPTR) = J2;
      RETURN(YES);
   END;
   IF TRY(I2, J2, I2, J2-1) THEN
      RETURN(YES);
   IF TRY(I2, J2, I2+1, J2) THEN
      RETURN(YES);
   IF TRY(I2, J2, I2, J2+1) THEN
      RETURN(YES);
   IF TRY(I2, J2, I2-1, J2) THEN
      RETURN(YES);
   PATHPTR = PATHPTR - 1;
   RETURN(NO);
END TRY;

PRINTPATH: PROCEDURE;
   STATE(*, *) = 'X';
   DO I = 1 TO PATHPTR;
      STATE(IPATH(I), JPATH(I)) = ' ';
   END;
   PUT SKIP(2) EDIT (((STATE(I,J) DO J = 1 TO N) DO I = 1 TO M))
      (COLUMN(1), (N)A(1));
END PRINTPATH;

END MOUSE;
```

There is no claim that we went directly from original conception to final working PL/I without a single slip. But it is true that most of our mistakes were made
with pseudo-code, and corrected long before the program made it into PL/I, let
alone onto a machine. At each stage of the process, it was easy to analyze, test, and
revise, because the program structure was clearly expressed as a handful of routines
and a few lines of code, not a hundred lines of PL/I.

The maze program is pretty big; it takes effort to analyze. Yet our version has
fewer statements than the original, and is far easier to understand. This is not
because we have better comments, nor is it because our identifiers are more meaningful. The main difference is structural.

We chose our control structures on the basis of legibility; people tend to understand them with little effort. Our version of the maze program has only one label
besides procedure names. That in itself is no great accomplishment, but it indicates
that the flow of control must be essentially from top to bottom.

The biggest change we made was to break the job into five small functions, each one of which can be assimilated separately, then treated as a black box that does some part of the job. Once it works, we need no longer concern ourselves with *how* it does something, only with the fact that it does. We thus have some assurance that we can deal with the program a small section at a time without much concern for the rest of the code. There is no other way to retain control of a large program.

Write and test a big program in small pieces.

Recursion represents no saving of time or storage. Somewhere in the computer must be maintained a list of all the places a recursive routine is called, so the program can eventually find its way back. But the storage for that list is shared among many different uses. More important, it is managed automatically; many of the burdens of storage management and control flow are placed on the compiler, not on the programmer. And since bookkeeping details are hidden, the program can be much easier to understand. Learning to think recursively takes some effort, but it is repaid with smaller and simpler programs.

Not every problem benefits from a recursive approach, but those that deal with data that is recursively defined often lead to very complicated programs unless the code is also recursive. A list, for example, can be said to consist of two elements, where each element is either an atom or a list. To trace through an arbitrary list requires an indefinite amount of storage to keep track of how to get back. The recursion mechanism provides this simply and concisely.

Even if you cannot use recursion in such a situation, perhaps because you must stick to Fortran, or because it is too inefficient (don't believe that until you've tried it), you will find it valuable to do the original design as a recursive program. Then unfold the recursion, simulating the recursive storage with your own explicitly indexed data structures. The resulting program should be cleaner and easier to understand than if you start from scratch.

Use recursive procedures for recursively-defined data structures.

The discipline of breaking a large job into appropriate small pieces is often called "structured design" and sometimes "composite design." Whatever you choose to call it, that discipline is necessary. To summarize some of the points made in this chapter about program structure,

(1) The only way to write and maintain a big program is as a set of small functions, subroutines, or procedures. No module should have to know much about the total problem, nor deal with more than a handful of immediate neighbors.

(2) Each module should deal with but one aspect of the solution, for otherwise it will become too big and too complicated. If a module does precisely one job, then it will not become a tangle of pieces lumped arbitrarily, nor will it be simply a displaced fragment of some other module.

(3) A module should hide from its fellows the details of how it performs its task, for otherwise one module cannot be changed independently of others.

POINTS TO PONDER

4.1   The function

```
INTEGER FUNCTION TEST(BOARD,I,J)
INTEGER BOARD(8,8)
TEST = -1
IF (I.LT.1 .OR. I.GT.8 .OR. J.LT.1 .OR. J.GT.8) RETURN
IF (BOARD(I,J).GE.0 .AND. BOARD(I,J).LE.4) TEST = BOARD(I,J)
RETURN
END
```

returns −1 if BOARD(I,J) is undefined or illegal; otherwise it returns BOARD(I,J). Rewrite subroutine STORE of the checker-playing program to use TEST. Add code to SEARCH to include valid single jumping moves. At most eight statements should have to be added. (Don't forget to add TEST to the INTEGER statement and increase the sizes of ROW and COL.) What would be involved in adding jumps to the original version?

4.2   What simplifications can be made in the checker-playing subroutines if we use a 10 by 10 checkerboard, where the border squares contain negative values?

4.3   What happens to the original maze program if the top border looks like

```
...010...
...000...
.........
```

What if the top left corner looks like

```
110......
000......
.........
```

The POINT array can handle up to 60 loops. Can you define a maze that has more than 60 loops? Remember that

```
..............
111111111111111
010101010101010
000000000000000
```

looks like seven loops when searched from left to right. Does our version handle these cases correctly?

4.4   Rewrite the maze program without using recursion, using the recursive version as a model. How much bigger and more complicated does it get? Can you do better with a different approach?

4.5 In the first edition of this book, we presented the following version of the maze program. In retrospect, we don't much care for it. Criticize it, and contrast it with the recursive version.

```
/*    MOUSE IN A MAZE    */
/* SEARCHES PERIPHERY OF AN M X N MATRIX (MAX 50 X 50)   */
/* FOR AN ENTRY POINT.  THEN FOLLOWS PATH BY SIMULATING  */
/* MAN WITH RIGHT HAND ON WALL (TURN RIGHT IF YOU CAN,   */
/* LEFT IF YOU MUST) UNTIL HE REEMERGES.  FIRST PATH     */
/* WITH EXIT DIFFERENT THAN ENTRANCE IS ACCEPTED.        */
/* MAZE='1'B IS A PATH, MAZE='0'B IS A WALL.             */

EX510: PROCEDURE OPTIONS (MAIN);

/*** CONSTANTS ***/
   DECLARE (UP INITIAL(0), LEFT INITIAL(1),
           DOWN INITIAL(2), RIGHT INITIAL(3))
      STATIC FIXED BINARY;

/*** GLOBAL VARIABLES ***/
   DECLARE MAZE(50,50) BIT(1),
           (XPOS, YPOS)(1250) FIXED BINARY,
           L FIXED BINARY;

   ON ENDFILE STOP;

/*** INPUT AND LIST MAZE ***/
MORE:
   GET LIST (M, N);
   IF M<2 | M>50 | N<2 | N>50 THEN DO;
      PUT SKIP LIST (M, N, 'BAD DIMENSIONS');  STOP;
                                   END;

   GET EDIT (((MAZE(I,J) DO J = 1 TO N) DO I = 1 TO M))
      (COLUMN(1), (N)B(1));
   PUT PAGE EDIT (((MAZE(I,J) DO J = 1 TO N) DO I = 1 TO M))
      (LINE(33-M/2), (M)(COLUMN(40-N/2), (N)B(1)));

/*** SEARCH PERIPHERY ***/
   DECLARE FIND ENTRY (FIXED BINARY, FIXED BINARY, FIXED BINARY)
           RETURNS (BIT(1));          /* '1'B IF PATH FOUND */

   DO K = 2 TO M-1;
      IF FIND(K,1,RIGHT) THEN GOTO FOUND;
      IF FIND(K,N,LEFT)  THEN GOTO FOUND;
   END;
   DO K = 2 TO N-1;
      IF FIND(1,K,DOWN) THEN GOTO FOUND;
      IF FIND(M,K,UP)   THEN GOTO FOUND;
   END;

   PUT SKIP LIST ('NO ENTRANCE');  GOTO MORE;


/*** PRINT ANSWER ***/
   DECLARE XMAZE(50,50) CHARACTER(1);

FOUND:
   XMAZE = 'X';

   DO J = 1 TO L;          /* L, XPOS, YPOS ARE SET IN FIND */
      XMAZE(XPOS(J),YPOS(J)) = ' ';
   END;
   PUT PAGE EDIT (((XMAZE(I,J) DO J = 1 TO N) DO I = 1 TO M))
      (LINE(33-M/2), (M)(COLUMN(40-N/2), (N)A(1)));
   GOTO MORE;
```

```
/*   PROCEDURE FOR SEARCHING:  */
/* BEGINS AT BORDER CELL KX,KY AND PROBES IN DIRECTION    */
/* KW.  IF ENTRY THERE THEN FOLLOWS PATH, AND RETURNS     */
/* '1'B IF COMES OUT SOMEWHERE ELSE.                      */
/* STORES L ELEMENTS OF PATH IN XPOS, YPOS                */

   FIND:  PROCEDURE (KX, KY, KW) RETURNS (BIT(1));

   /*** CONSTANTS ***/
      DECLARE (DX(0:3) INITIAL(-1,0,1,0), DY(0:3) INITIAL(0,-1,0,1))
        STATIC FIXED BINARY;

   /*** STORAGE ***/
      DECLARE (X, Y, W) FIXED BINARY;

      IF MAZE(KX,KY) = '0'B | MAZE(KX+DX(KW),KY+DY(KW)) = '0'B
         THEN RETURN ('0'B);

   /*** EXPLORE ***/
      XPOS(1) = KX;  YPOS(1) = KY;
      XPOS(2),X = KX+DX(KW);   YPOS(2),Y = KY+DY(KW);
      W = KW;  L = 2;

      DO WHILE (X>1 & X<M & Y>1 & Y<N);
         W = MOD(W+3,4);                          /* TURN RIGHT */

         DO WHILE (MAZE(X+DX(W),Y+DY(W)) = '0'B);
            W = MOD(W+1,4);         /* TURN LEFT UNTIL OUT */
         END;

         L = L+1;
         XPOS(L),X = X+DX(W);   YPOS(L),Y = Y+DY(W);

         DO J = L-2 TO 1 BY -1;                   /* TEST FOR KNOT */
            IF X = XPOS(J) & Y = YPOS(J) THEN
               IF J = 1 THEN RETURN ('0'B);
               ELSE DO;
                  L = J;   GOTO EXIT;
                     END;
         END;
   EXIT:
      END;

      RETURN ('1'B);                      /* REACHED BORDER */
   END FIND;

END EX510;
```

From *Computerworld*, June, 1972:

Slip of the Keypuncher's Finger Means
City to Lose $290,000 in Tax Revenue

WOONSOCKET, R.I. — A keypunch error compounded by a lack of programming safeguards will cost this city almost $300,000 in tax revenues this year.

The error occurred several weeks ago when the city's tax evaluation was being computed. It caused a 1967 Ford to be valued at over $7 million — $7,000,950 to be exact — and therefore cause the tax rate to be based on a figure that was about $7 million too high.

As a result, tax revenues will be decreased by $290,000, reported A. Robert Mailloux, finance director. The city will not increase the tax rate, so department heads will have to "pull in the belt," Mailloux said.

The error resulted when operators were preparing a test run for the property tax rolls on the municipal card-fed Honeywell 110. A keypunch operator mistakenly punched a "P" in the first column of a seven-column field.

The first four columns should have been empty, indicating that the automobile was only worth $950.

The logic of the computer, Mailloux related, stripped the zone bit from the field during a multiplication operation. The letter was thereby translated into a "7" and the next three blanks were filled with zeroes by the computer.

$182 Million Correct

The result, then, was $7,000,950 instead of $950 for the automobile; the total tax assessment for the city was originally reported as $187 million, based on an 80% rate, instead of the correct $182 million, Mailloux confirmed.

Tax revenues will be proportionately reduced, he added.

There were five checkpoints at which the erroneous card should have been detected and destroyed, he continued. In fact, the error was detected, and a new card punched, but the old card was not removed from the deck, despite the fact that a supervisor reported that it had been removed and destroyed.

Mailloux said the program should have contained checks that would not have permitted so great an assessment on an automobile to be processed.

A preparatory run by account number (taxpayer number) and another preparatory run by automobile registration number both should have detected the duplicate card, he related.

There were, however, "no programming safeguards," he stated. "Given human frailties, the program was the ultimate chance" to detect and avoid the error, he added.

The error was discovered two weeks ago, when the tax bills were mailed and the owner of the Ford received a bill for $290,000. Officials would not identify the recipient.

The error marks the "largest financial error in the city's history," according to local sources. Other observers suggested the $290,000 sum represented the largest amount ever lost, without compensation or recovery, for a computer-related error.

The actual loss will be increased if the city has to borrow money between now and the end of the fiscal year.

In twenty-five words or less, this article says that the assessment program did its computation without checking that its input data made sense. There is a lesson here that every programmer must learn, usually the hard way (how would you like to be the programmer who wrote the assessment program?) and often several times: NEVER TRUST ANY DATA. Input prepared by people or even by other programs will contain errors. A good program tests its input for validity (the letter "P" is not a digit) and, in critical cases like tax computations, for plausibility. (An automobile assessed at seven million dollars is not plausible.)

Many introductory programming texts contain variants of the problem "Write a program to read three numbers A, B, and C, representing the sides of a triangle, and compute the area of the triangle." Here is one solution:

```
      READ (5, 23) A, B, C
   23 FORMAT (3F10.0)
      S = (A + B + C) / 2.0
      AREA = SQRT(S * (S - A) * (S - B) * (S - C))
      WRITE (6, 17) A, B, C, AREA
   17    FORMAT (1P4E16.7)
      STOP
      END
```

In most ways this is a good program: it is well-formatted, and copies its input data to the output for visual inspection. The output format is well chosen: it uses the E format to handle very large or very small answers without losing significant digits, and the scale factor 1P to print one position before the decimal point, so the answers are in the form most familiar to readers. Our only minor complaint concerns the apparently random statement numbers.

But what happens if we test the program on the "triangle" (3, 1, 1)? Most probable is an unexpected termination with a diagnostic like "negative argument in SQRT," certainly an indirect way to report that the input does not represent a triangle. (And try it on −1, −1, −1.)

You should always "launder" your input: after S has been computed, verify that no side is too big (or negative). One programmer used PL/I's built-in function ANY to test each element of an array T which contains the lengths of the three sides:

```
        S = SUM(T)/2;
    IF ANY(T <=0)|ANY(T>S) THEN    it's not a triangle ...

    IF ANY(T=S) THEN    it's a straight line ...
        . . .
```

The test for a straight line may not always be reliable, for reasons we shall explore in Chapter 6, but the generally suspicious approach is commendable. This checking is easy in PL/I. In Fortran, the same tests require more code, which may explain why they are not often made.

Test input for validity and plausibility.

Simple tests save later grief. Does the program read a parameter to define an array size? Then test that it does not exceed the array bounds. Here is part of a sort program:

```
      DIMENSION X(300)
C     READ NUMBERS TO BE SORTED.
      READ 1,N,(X(I),I=1,N)
    1 FORMAT(I3/(F5.1))
C     INITIALIZE TO MAKE N-1 COMPARISONS ON FIRST PASS.
      K=N-1
C     INITIALIZE TO BEGIN COMPARISONS WITH THE FIRST 2 NUMBERS.
    6 J=1
C     L IS USED TO RECORD THE FACT THAT AN INTERCHANGE OCCURS.
   19 L=0
C     MAKE COMPARISONS.
      DO 2 I=J,K
      IF(X(I)-X(I+1)) 2,2,3
    3 ...
```

There are minor flaws, such as the random statement numbers (again) and the use of an arithmetic IF where a logical IF would be more readable, but we will defer discussion of the full text until Chapter 7. For now, let us concentrate on the input statement.

Suppose N exceeds 300. Parts of storage outside the array X may be overwritten. Whatever happens after that will not be good, nor will it tell the user unequivocally what he did wrong. The program may run to completion, but if the user does not look carefully at the output, he may not even notice that the program failed.

Some compilers (WATFIV, PL/I with SUBSCRIPTRANGE enabled, for instance) allow a check during execution that subscripts do not exceed array dimensions. This is a help, but not sufficient. First, many programmers do not use such compilers because "They're not efficient." (Presumably this means that it is vital to get the wrong answers quickly.) Second, subscript range checking will not detect the other deficiency in this code. Suppose that the value of N is one. Then the program compares X(1) with X(2), which is not defined and hence garbage. If the garbage happens to be less than X(1), X(1) is gone forever, since it is sorted out of its position.

If we write a precise description of the *exact* input data for which the sort program works, we find, of course, that it fails for N outside the range 2 to 300. At that point, we might be embarrassed into making it do something sensible for all values of N:

```
      DIMENSION X(300)
      READ 10, N
   10 FORMAT(I3)
      IF (N.LT.1 .OR. N.GT.300)    take error action
      READ 20, (X(I), I=1,N)
   20 FORMAT(F5.0)
      IF (N.EQ.1)    leave routine, since in order
      ...
```

It may be easier to redo a program than to describe *exactly* what cases it works for. In any case, writing the description should point to bugs, and to areas for improvement. (The author of this sort program came close — his second and third comments both suggest that there might not be two items.)

Make sure input cannot violate the limits of the program.

The statement
```
READ 1,N,(X(I),I=1,N)
```
in the sort program illustrates a risky way to read data. N has to be computed by the user, probably by hand. Since people make mistakes, this is an error-prone operation, especially if N is at all large. And while the statement is compact, it does not leave room for the checking that is so important with this form of input. It should be avoided.

As we said before, computers count better than people; let them do the work. Mark the end of the data, then read until the marker is encountered. (In some languages, the marker can be implicit, as in the
```
ON ENDFILE ... ;
```
statement of PL/I or the END=... construction in many Fortrans.) You would be annoyed if you had to count the number of cards in your source programs; thus compilers read until they find an END card or no more input. Do the same for *your* users.

Terminate input by end-of-file or marker, not by count.

The program below reads cards containing a name and a hair color, and totals the number of people with each color of hair.
```
      INTEGER NAME,COLOR,LAST,COL(6),COUNT(6)
      DATA COL/3HBLA,3HBLU,3HBRO,3HGRE,3HRED,3HWHI/,
     1 LAST,COUNT/4H0000,6*0/
    1 READ(5,2)NAME,COLOR
    2 FORMAT(A4,15X,A3)
      DO 3 I = 1,6
    3 IF( COLOR.EQ.COL(I) ) COUNT(I) = COUNT(I) + 1
      IF(NAME .NE. LAST) GO TO 1
      WRITE(6,4)
    4 FORMAT(12H COLOR COUNT)
      DO 5 I = 1,6
    5 WRITE(6,6)COL(I),COUNT(I)
    6 FORMAT(4X,A3,2X,I3)
      STOP
      END
```
Instead of forcing users to count their data cards correctly, the program uses an explicit "end-of-file" test — a card with a name field of "0000" marks the end of the input. Excellent! But notice that the end-of-file test is made only *after* the data from the end-of-file marker card has been checked and accumulated. Should a color

be punched in the "unused" field of the end-of-file card, it will corrupt the counts. This code may not fail often, but it is careless.

The use of mnemonics like "RED" and "BLU" instead of numeric codes like "1" and "2" is commendable, for it makes the program easier to use correctly. But if a color does not match any of the list, it is quietly skipped. Debugging input data is as important as debugging a program — some provision for locating bad input should be included. In this case, each bad color should be printed (with an indication of which card is in error, for the deck may contain hundreds of cards.)

The program "works", but with negligible effort it can be improved:

```
      INTEGER NAME, COLOR, LAST, COL(6), COUNT(6), CARDNO
      DATA COL(1), COL(2), COL(3) /'BLA', 'BLU', 'BRO'/
      DATA COL(4), COL(5), COL(6) /'GRE', 'RED', 'WHI'/
      DATA LAST /'0000'/
      DO 10 I = 1,6
         COUNT(I) = 0
   10 CONTINUE
      CARDNO = 0
   20 READ(5,21) NAME, COLOR
   21 FORMAT(A4, 15X, A3)
      IF (NAME .EQ. LAST) GOTO 50
         CARDNO = CARDNO + 1
         DO 30 I = 1,6
            IF (COLOR .NE. COL(I)) GOTO 30
               COUNT(I) = COUNT(I) + 1
               GOTO 40
   30    CONTINUE
C FALL OUT IF BAD COLOR
         WRITE(6,31) COLOR, CARDNO
   31    FORMAT(' BAD COLOR - ', A3, ' IN CARD NUMBER', I5)
   40    GOTO 20
C END OF DATA INPUT
   50 WRITE(6,51) (COL(I), COUNT(I), I = 1,6)
   51 FORMAT(4X, A3, I5)
      STOP
      END
```

We have written the input loop as a large DO-WHILE (while the NAME is not equal to LAST). If a color is recognized, we count it and skip to the next case (GOTO 40 is an early exit from the loop); otherwise we list the bad input color and then loop.

Identify bad input; recover if possible.

The same error, treating the end-of-file marker as legitimate data, is carried a step further in this program for computing student grade averages:

```
...
I=1;
/* INITIALIZE SUM */
IN: SUM=0;
/* READ SCORES AND COMPUTE SUM */
DO J=1 BY 1 TO 5;
GET LIST (SCORE(I,J));
SUM=SUM+SCORE(I,J);
END;
/* STOP READING IF FIRST SCORE IS NEGATIVE */
IF SCORE(I,1)<0 THEN GO TO OUT;
/* COMPUTE AVERAGE */
AVG(I)=SUM/5;
/* READ NAME */
GET LIST (NAME(I));
I=I+1;
/* GET NEXT STUDENT'S SCORES */
GO TO IN;
/* COMPUTE TOTAL NUMBER OF STUDENTS */
OUT: I=I-1;
/* PRINT ... */
...
```

The comments imply that scores and names are read until the first score is negative; this indicates the end of data. Unfortunately, what comments imply is not always precisely what happens. Because GET LIST reads free-form input, this program requires *five dummy scores* to terminate the DO loop that reads scores, although only the first need be negative. If less than five are given, the program encounters the end of the input unexpectedly, before the GET LIST is satisfied. Since no ENDFILE action has been specified, the program simply terminates without printing the desired output. This is not implied by the comments.

PL/I's explicit test for end-of-file is much superior to the Fortran-like mechanism used here. Let us use it to correct the error. One possibility is

```
ON ENDFILE
    GOTO OUT;

DO I = 1 TO IMAX;   /* LOOP UNTIL EOF OR ARRAYS FULL */
    GET LIST (SCORE(I,*), NAME(I));
        should check data for validity here
    AVG(I) = SUM(SCORE(I,*))/5;
END;
    get here if arrays are full

OUT:
    output processing
```

(A * subscript repeats an operation over all legal values of that subscript. Thus GET LIST (SCORE(I,*)) reads SCORE(I,1), SCORE(I,2), etc.; SUM(SCORE(I,*)) adds them all up.) We have dispensed with the negative dummy score for terminating the input. As an added bonus, we can easily avoid reading more input than the arrays can hold, by limiting the range of the DO loop that replaces

```
I=1;
IN:
   ...
I=I+1;
GO TO IN;
```

The `ENDFILE` condition provides an early exit from this loop, so if we fall out of the loop, we know there is too much data for the program to handle. We also used a `GOTO` in the `ON ENDFILE` statement, rather than placing the output code there itself, so we could keep the code laid out in the order in which it is obeyed. So long as the input routine is not too large, there is little danger of confusion.

One can also use the `ON ENDFILE` unit just to set a flag, which is then tested after each attempt to read. This organization requires no branching.

```
ON ENDFILE
   EOF = YES;
EOF = NO;
GET LIST (...);
IF EOF = NO THEN
   normal processing
```

In either case, the intent is to make end of file look to the rest of the program as much as possible like any other input record. We will return to this topic again later in the chapter.

Treat end of file conditions in a uniform manner.

Explicit tests for end of file and the identification of faulty data make programs easier for people to use. So does input that is easy to prepare correctly:

From *Computerworld*, October, 1971:

Loss of One Digit Brings School Scheduling Snafu

KINGSTON, MASS. — One lost column in a punched card caused several high school classes to be scheduled for one room, while scores of other students wandered aimlessly all day long, for lack of a destination.

That's the description given by local and wire service reports of a computerized scheduling snafu at Silver Lake Regional High School here, but employees of the school "didn't know we had a big problem until we read about it in the paper."

There actually were some problems, originally blamed on keypunch errors, but they were not as severe as reported.

Assistant Superintendant Norman Donegan claimed the school committee was "not particularly upset" at the problems, which were reportedly settled in two or three days.

The matter has not been dropped, but there is no intense investigation either. Donegan indicated that the company involved in the error may lose the computer contract, which is worth $2000 a year, but that "we don't plan to stop scheduling by computer.

"In fact, we've even thought about increasing" the applications, he stated.

Donegan said that the error apparently was caused when the first digit in a three column field was dropped. The field indicates Teacher-Department-Subject, and with the omission of the teacher, the other categories became jumbled.

In other instances, the teacher indicated had left the school system, causing scheduling problems for students if a replacement had not been hired.

Leaving aside any question of why the program failed to check its input, this "minor" problem might never have happened if input formats were better suited to humans, and if mnemonics were used. Mnemonics make it easier for people to remember legal input and understand output, and they make it less likely that a keypunch error will transform one legal code into another one.

To illustrate, here is a part of a program which computes prices of metals of various types and weights:

```
      ...
      KOUNT = 0
 1    READ 6,WEIGHT,XMETAL
 6    FORMAT(F10.1,3X,F4.1)
      KOUNT = KOUNT+1
      DATA BRAC1/0./,BRAC2/1000./,BRAC3/2000./,BRAC4/3000./,BRAC5/4000./
      DATA ALUM/1./,TIN/2./,COPPER/3./,BORON/4./
      IF(WEIGHT.LE.BRAC1)GO TO 100
      IF(WEIGHT.LT.BRAC2.AND.XMETAL.EQ.ALUM)GO TO 101
      IF(WEIGHT.LT.BRAC3.AND.XMETAL.EQ.ALUM)GO TO 102
      ...
      IF(WEIGHT.LT.BRAC3.AND.XMETAL.EQ.BORON)GO TO 118
      IF(WEIGHT.LT.BRAC4.AND.XMETAL.EQ.BORON)GO TO 119
      IF(WEIGHT.GE.BRAC5.AND.XMETAL.EQ.BORON)GO TO 120
      METAL=XMETAL
100   PRINT 200,WEIGHT,METAL,KOUNT
200   FORMAT(1X,9HWEIGHT = ,F10.1,8HMETAL = ,I2,27HERROR FOUND IN CARD N
     1UMBER I3)
      GO TO 1
101   COST=WEIGHT*3.00
      GO TO 300
102   COST=WEIGHT*2.75
      GO TO 300
      ...
118   COST=WEIGHT*1.50
      GO TO 300
119   COST=WEIGHT*1.25
      GO TO 300
120   COST=WEIGHT*1.00
300   METAL=XMETAL
      PRINT 301,KOUNT,METAL,WEIGHT,COST
301   FORMAT(1X,13HSHIPMENT NO. (,I2,1H),3X,7HMETAL= ,I2,3X,9HWEIGHT = ,F
     110.1,3X,7HCOST = ,F10.2)
      GO TO 1
```

Each input data card contains a weight and a numeric code for a metal. In all, there are twenty IF's to determine the weight bracket and metal to use for computation, and twenty different computations (statement numbers 101 through 120). Clearly, it would be better to put the prices in an array, indexed by metal type and weight class, and in fact the textbook from which the example was taken later gives a version of the program that does just that.

There are some other minor things to criticize. For instance, it is error-prone and inflexible to use a source card right up to the last column, as in statements 200 and 301. FORMAT 200, for example, leaves no space between the metal code and the word "ERROR". To fix this buglet, we must change both statement 200 and its continuation, then we must correct the character count (27) as well. If instead the card broke to a continuation at the end of a field, this problem would not arise, and only one change would be needed to fix the error:

```
 200 FORMAT(1X, 'WEIGHT = ', F10.1, '  METAL = ', I2,
     $   '  ERROR FOUND IN CARD NUMBER ', I3)
```

The program has good points, too. It counts its data cards, instead of relying on the user. It copies the input onto the output (after computation) so it can be inspected visually. And, most important, it validates its input, testing for negative or zero weight and invalid metal code. It prints the offending card and its sequence number, then continues to the next data.

But our enthusiasm is tempered by discovering that if a negative or zero weight is encountered, the program prints the value of METAL for the *previous* input card. Label 100 is placed incorrectly, one statement too late.

If the conversion

```
     METAL = XMETAL
```

were done once, immediately after the READ, the bug would vanish, and so would the need for statement 300 and the one before statement 100.

The other, more general, failing is the use of numeric codes (floating point at that) to name the metals. (Was floating point used because all the metals had names that were "floating point" variables in Fortran? What if we added LEAD, NICKEL, and IRON?) A typical line of output looks like

```
     SHIPMENT NO.( 1)   METAL= 1   WEIGHT =    1000.0  COST =    2750.00
```

It is only after scanning the listing that we can deduce that metal 1 is aluminum.

The use of numeric codes is bad practice in a program that people use directly. The codes in this program are not even in alphabetical order. How can a user remember them? (As we mentioned, the textbook presents another version of this program a few pages later, which uses alphabetic names instead of numeric codes for the metals, but discards all error checking.)

Make input easy to prepare and output self-explanatory.

Here is an example that shows ill-chosen mnemonic values:

Write a program segment that will assign sales area 1 to each even salesman, and sales area 2 to each odd salesman.

```
     DIMENSION SALESM(17)
     DO 20 IJ=1,17
  10 IF(IJ/2*2-IJ) 12,11,12
  11 SALESM(IJ)=1.
     GO TO 20
  12 SALESM(IJ)=2.
  20 CONTINUE
```

The curious expression IJ/2*2-IJ is a Fortran idiom that determines whether IJ is evenly divisible by two. The original problem can be solved more clearly and succinctly with the MOD function:

```
      DIMENSION SALESM(17)
      DO 20 I = 1, 17
         SALESM(I) = MOD(I,2) + 1
   20 CONTINUE
```

We are more concerned here with the mnemonic values chosen: even-numbered salesmen have an odd number, while odd-numbered salesmen have an even number. This is backwards. It is certainly no more difficult to let "1" be the code for odd-numbered salesmen, and "2" the code for even. (We leave it to the reader to decide whether using a floating point array to hold integer values is an appropriate data representation.)

Programs should not only cope with incorrect input, but also encourage users to make fewer errors by being easy to use. Consider this input fragment:

```
      READ(1,4) XIHP(I),R(I),FORCE(I),NREV(I)
    4 FORMAT(F5.1,F3.1,F3.0,I2)
```

If you are an occasional user of this program, will you be able to remember, a week from now, that the XIHP field is five columns wide, R and FORCE are three, and NREV is two? Not likely. There would be less to remember if the author had used a uniform format, like

```
    4 FORMAT(3F5.0, I5)
```

in which all fields have the same width. This also leaves room for future growth — whatever NREV is, it may someday be bigger than 99, which is all the I2 format permits. I2 is not only non-uniform, but restrictive.

You might even consider doing this:

```
      READ(1,4) XIHP(I), R(I), FORCE(I), REV
    4 FORMAT(4F5.0)
      NREV(I) = REV
```

Now we do not need to right-justify the integer NREV — we enter it with a decimal point like everything else, and convert it internally. (As it turns out, the only place in the program where NREV is used is in a long product where all the other factors are floating point. It might as well have been declared floating point anyway.)

The difference between F3.1 and F3.0, by the way, lies in the interpretation of an input number that does not contain a decimal point. If the number contains a decimal point, as it should for reliability, the explicit point overrides the decimal point position in the FORMAT statement. Floating point input specifications should thus be restricted to the form Fn.0. (We have quietly made this change in most of our examples so far.) Omitting decimal points to make fields smaller is penny-wise, pound-foolish.

Use uniform input formats.

While we are making uniform formats, consider this excerpt from a program in another text:

```
      READ (5,100) MAX,JLOW,JHIGH
100   FORMAT (I3,2I4)
      ...
      READ (5,7) N(I)
  7   FORMAT (I4)
      ...
```

Here two (randomly numbered) FORMAT statements are used, because the pointless irregularity in the first means that it cannot be used with the second READ. (Did the programmer use I3 because he "knew" that MAX would never exceed 999? Users now have to learn two formats; when the program grows, they may have to learn a third.) Do it this way:

```
      READ(5,100) MAX, JLOW, JHIGH
100   FORMAT(3I5)
      ...
      READ(5,100) N(I)
```

The idea is not to save the small space represented by a second FORMAT, but to make life simpler for the user. Even if you prefer to write FORMAT's after each I/O statement (a good practice), make them as similar as possible.

Formats should also be chosen with some thought to the probable device used to create input — usually a keypunch or a terminal. Free-form input is easiest; next best are uniform fields near the left end of the card or line. Imagine typing with this format, even after the missing comma is inserted:

```
      GET EDIT(X,ZILCH)(X(10),F(4)X(65),A(1));
```

If possible, numbers should be justified left, not right. (That was the purpose of our floating-to-fixed conversion above.) Spread the data out a little — cramming it into the absolute minimum space makes it too hard for reading by people, who may well have to look at it to find errors.

Make input easy to proofread.

The ideal arrangement for reading numbers, especially for getting programs working quickly, is free-form input, where the data layout is essentially unspecified.

Free-form input is easy in PL/I:

```
      GET LIST (A, B, C);
```

reads input until it finds three numbers. These can be on one card or line, or on several, separated by blanks or commas or card/line boundaries.

Not all Fortran implementations allow free-form input, but some, especially for interactive systems, do provide unrestricted input, often as

```
      READ A, B, C
```

You must weigh the question of future portability against ease of use right here and now. In this case, our vote goes to ease of use.

Use free-form input when possible.

The following READ statement sets five variables:

```
READ(1,10) KONST1,KONST2,FEED,DIAM,RPM
10 FORMAT(I6,I6,F5.3,F5.3,F4.0)
```

Suppose you had to use this program periodically (after negotiating to have the input format made more uniform). Without looking, is the third argument the feed rate or the diameter? If you last used the program a week ago, would you remember? When there are many (i.e., more than one or two) arguments or parameters to be provided to a program, let the users specify their parameters by name; that way they have to input only what they want changed from the default, and they don't have to remember any particular order.

Parameters can be read directly by name with the GET DATA statement of PL/I. Input like

```
FEED=27.0    DIAM=3.5    RPM=3600.0
```

lets users give input arguments in an arbitrary order and format, as long as they can remember what the names are. Fortran's NAMELIST feature does much the same thing, although it is nonstandard and its use is clumsy.

If input parameters are supplied by name, you can use default values in a graceful way. If some parameter is normally given a certain value, build that value into the program; then if users do not specify its value, they will get the built-in value "by default." Of course the defaults have to be chosen intelligently, to satisfy some significant fraction of the user population. On output reports, it may be helpful to print the defaulted values as well as the inputs, so the user will know what the program did. (We have also sometimes found it useful to print date and time, to help people identify their output.)

Use self-identifying input. Allow defaults.
Echo both on output.

In our version of the maze program of Chapter 4, you may recall that we wrote a separate function READMAZE to read each new maze, rather than embedding the input code in-line in the main routine. This allowed our main loop to be simply

```
DO WHILE (READMAZE() = YES);
    IF FINDPATH() = YES THEN
        CALL PRINTPATH;
    ELSE
        PUT SKIP(2) LIST ('NO PATH');
END;
```

All of the details of maze input are hidden from the main routine, including coping with end of file and invalid input. If READMAZE returns YES (actually '1'B) it found a maze, which is now ready to be processed. Otherwise it returns NO ($'0'$B) and the loop is finished.

As we have said several times, the hard part of programming is controlling complexity — keeping the pieces decoupled so they can be dealt with separately instead of all at once. And the need to separate into pieces is not some academically interesting point, but a practical necessity, to keep things from interacting with each other in unexpected ways.

Writing a separate input function is a prime example of decoupling, an example which crops up frequently. To illustrate, let us examine the following program, which reads text and computes the average number of words per sentence. It is not the most general program in the world, for the input comes on exactly ten cards, but this can be readily changed.

```
        DIMENSION IA(80)
        DATA IBLK,IPER/' ','.'/
        NWDS=0
        NSEN=0
        DO 7 I=1,10
        READ(5,1) IA
1       FORMAT(80A1)
        JW=0
        J=1
5       IF(IA(J).NE.IPER) GO TO 2
        IF(JW.NE.0) NWDS=NWDS+1
        NSEN=NSEN+1
        GO TO 3
2       IF(IA(J).EQ.IBLK) GO TO 4
        JW=1
        GO TO 3
4       IF(JW.EQ.1) NWDS=NWDS+1
        JW=0
3       J=J+1
        IF(J.LE.80) GO TO 5
7       IF(JW.EQ.1) NWDS=NWDS+1
        AVG=NWDS/NSEN
        WRITE(6,6) AVG
6       FORMAT('0AVERAGE WORDS PER SENTENCE =',F10.2)
        STOP
        END
```

The program is rather involved, mainly because the card-reading (with its accompanying tests for the end of the card) is thoroughly intertwined with counting the words and sentences. With this much complexity, it's not too surprising that the code is wrong — the average is always too high. (You might like to verify this.)

Suppose we separate fetching characters from counting interesting things. Following the lead of the maze program, we define a function READCH which will read the next character from the input. READCH should take care of all the nasty details of converting the 80 characters of a card (let us say) into 80 separate characters, handed out one at a time. It should also give back a signal that no more characters are left when the end of the input is reached.

Given READCH (which we'll write in a moment) the main program simplifies quite a bit. In pseudo-code,

```
inword = NO
nword = 0
nsent = 0
WHILE (readch(char) = YES)
   IF (char = blank)
      inword = NO
   ELSE IF (char = period)
      nsent = nsent + 1
   ELSE IF (inword = NO)
      inword = YES
      nword = nword + 1
IF (nsent > 0)
   print nword/nsent
```

This is just about right to verify that the underlying algorithm works, even for fairly perverse sequences of blanks, words and periods. Now we can translate it into Fortran.

```
      INTEGER READCH, BLANK, PERIOD, CHAR, YES
      DATA BLANK /' '/, PERIOD /'.'/, NO /0/, YES /1/
      NWORD = 0
      NSENT = 0
      INWORD = NO
   10 IF (READCH(CHAR) .EQ. NO) GOTO 90
         IF (CHAR .EQ. BLANK) INWORD = NO
         IF (CHAR .EQ. PERIOD) NSENT = NSENT + 1
         IF (CHAR .EQ. BLANK .OR. CHAR .EQ. PERIOD) GOTO 20
         IF (INWORD .EQ. YES) GOTO 20
            INWORD = YES
            NWORD = NWORD + 1
   20    GOTO 10
   90 IF (NSENT .GT. 0) AVG = FLOAT(NWORD) / FLOAT(NSENT)
      IF (NSENT .LE. 0) AVG = 0.0
      WRITE(6,91) AVG
   91    FORMAT('0', 'AVERAGE WORDS PER SENTENCE =', F10.2)
      STOP
      END
```

Now the only remaining detail is READCH. Although there are several ways to write it, they all share the same basic approach — read in a whole card, then dole out the characters one at a time, reading a new card whenever the current one is exhausted. As a matter of timing, it's easier to read a new card only when it is really needed, not when the old one has just run out. Also, since READCH really returns two things, we return the character in the argument, and the end of file signal as the function value. This approach seems most convenient for Fortran, and eliminates the problem of choosing an end of file signal that is not a valid character.

```
      INTEGER FUNCTION READCH(CHAR)
      INTEGER LINE(81), NEXTCH, CHAR, YES, NO
      DATA NEXTCH /82/, LINE(81) /' '/, YES /1/, NO /0/
C
      IF (NEXTCH .LE. 81) GOTO 20
         READ(5,11,END=90) (LINE(I), I=1,80)
   11       FORMAT(80A1)
         NEXTCH = 1
   20 CHAR = LINE(NEXTCH)
      NEXTCH = NEXTCH + 1
      READCH = YES
      RETURN
C END OF FILE
   90 READCH = NO
      RETURN
      END
```

The construction END=90 in the READ statement causes a branch to statement 90 when end of file occurs. This feature is well on its way to becoming a standard. (It is part of Fortran 77.) We have also assumed that the end of a card should mark the end of a word. To ensure this, READCH returns a blank after the end of each card. (Notice that this is done with a well-chosen data structure: there is a dummy 81st column on the card which is always blank. READCH fetches a new card only after this blank has been returned.)

There are some pragmatic advantages to having a separate function for input, many of which we discussed in Chapter 4. Most important is simply breaking a big job into smaller, non-interacting pieces. Furthermore, I/O is often the most system-dependent part of a program; when a program has to be moved or changed, it's *much* better to have all input and output in one place than scattered randomly throughout a large program. As another benefit, consider how easy it is to implement centralized functions like stripping off trailing blanks or performing character set translations.

Localize input and output in subroutines.

Input/output is the interface between a program and its environment. Two rules govern all I/O programming: NEVER TRUST ANY DATA, and REMEMBER THE USER. This requires that a program be as foolproof as is reasonably possible, so that it behaves intelligently even when used incorrectly, and that it be easy to use correctly. Ask yourself: Will it defend itself against the stupidity and ignorance of its users (including myself)? Would I want to have to use it myself?

To summarize the major principles discussed in this chapter:

(1) Check input data for validity and plausibility.

(2) Make sure that data does not violate limitations of the program.

("Garbage in, garbage out" is not a law of nature, but a commentary on how well principles (1) and (2) are followed in practice.)

(3) Read input until end-of-file or marker, not by count.

(4) Identify input errors and recover if possible. Do not stop on the first error. Do not simply ignore errors.

(5) Use mnemonic input and output. Make input easy to prepare (and easy to prepare correctly). Echo the input and any defaults onto the output; make output self-explanatory.

(6) Localize I/O instead of spreading it all over the program. Hide the details of end of file, buffering, etc., in functions.

(7) Make sure that program structure reflects the data the program processes.

POINTS TO PONDER

5.1   Write a free-form input subroutine that works from a pre-specified array of variable names. How much more work is required to allow for defaults? Once you have such a subroutine, how much harder is it to input variables of different types (say INTEGER as well as REAL variables)? How much harder is it to input elements of an array?

5.2   Here is a routine that does part of the job suggested in the previous problem — it converts characters into integers. Improve its structure.

```
          DIMENSION IDIG(10),IA(80)
          DATA IBLK,IDIG,IPLS,IMIN/' ','0','1','2','3','4','5','6','7','8','
         19','+','-'/
          READ(5,1) IA
 1        FORMAT(80A1)
          IDG=0
          NUM=0
          J=0
 3        J=J+1
          IF(J.GT.80) GO TO 2
          IF(IA(J).EQ.IBLK) GO TO 3
          IS=+1
          IF(IA(J).NE.IMIN) GO TO 4
          IS=-1
          J=J+1
          GO TO 5
 4        IF(IA(J).EQ.IPLS) J=J+1
 5        IF(J.GT.80) GO TO 6
          DO 7 I=1,10
          IF(IA(J).EQ.IDIG(I)) GO TO 8
 7        CONTINUE
          IF(IA(J).NE.IBLK) GO TO 9
          IF(IDG.EQ.0) GO TO 9
 12       NUM=NUM*IS
          WRITE(6,10) NUM
 10       FORMAT('0VALUE =',I10)
          STOP
 2        WRITE(6,11)
 11       FORMAT('0BLANK CARD')
          STOP
 6        IF(IDG.NE.0) GO TO 12
 9        WRITE(6,13) IA,J
 13       FORMAT(6X,80A1/6X,'INVALID CHARACTER NEAR COLUMN',I3)
          STOP
 8        NUM=NUM*10+I-1
          IDG=1
          J=J+1
          GO TO 5
          END
```

5.3   Fortran ignores most blanks in program statements, but treats most blanks as zeros in input data. Thus

```
      READ(5,10) N
   10 FORMAT(I5)
      IF (N .EQ. 1 024) WRITE(6,20) N
   20 FORMAT(1X, I5)
```

will cause the input number

```
      1 024
```

to be stored as 10024 by the READ statement, but compared to 1024 in the IF. Can you think of any benefit to be gained from this inconsistency? How can you avoid any trouble it might cause?

5.4   The following PL/I program counts words and sentences and computes averages. Debug it, then revise it along the lines suggested in this chapter.

```
            DECLARE   TEXT   CHARACTER(200) VARYING,
                      CHAR   CHARACTER(1),
                      (SENT,  /* NO. OF SENTENCES */
                      WORDS, /* NO. OF WORDS */
                      LETTERS)  FIXED ;

   START:   /* INITIALIZE AND READ TEXT */
            SENT, WORDS, LETTERS = 0 ;
            GET LIST( TEXT ) ;

            /* EXAMINE TEXT FOR WORDS AND SENTENCES, AND
               COUNT LETTERS IN THE PROCESS */

            DO I = 1 BY 1 TO LENGTH( TEXT ) ;
               CHAR = SUBSTR( TEXT, I, 1 ) ;
               IF CHAR='.' THEN
                  DO ;
                     /* A PERIOD ENDS A WORD AND A SENT. */
                     WORDS = WORDS + 1 ;
                     SENT = SENT + 1 ;
                  END ;
               ELSE IF CHAR=' ' THEN WORDS = WORDS + 1 ;
               ELSE   LETTERS = LETTERS + 1 ;

            /* NOTE THE ASSUMPTION THAT A CHARACTER IS
               CONSIDERED TO BE A LETTER IF IT IS NOT
               A PERIOD OR A BLANK. */

            END ;

            /* PRINT RESULTS */
            PUT SKIP EDIT( 'SENTENCES =', SENT,
                           'WORDS/SENTENCE =', WORDS/SENT,
                           'LETTERS/WORDS =', LETTERS/WORDS )
                         ( X(10), A, F(4) ) ;
            GO TO START ;
```

CHAPTER 6: **COMMON BLUNDERS**

A major concern of programming is making sure that a program can defend against bad data. But even with correct data, there is no guarantee that a program will work. In this chapter we will discuss other aspects of making software reliable.

We begin, appropriately enough, with initialization, for failing to set a variable to some value before using it is a fruitful source of error. For example:

```
      DOUBLE PRECISION FUNCTION SIN(X,E)
C     THIS DECLARATION COMPUTES SIN(X)TO ACCURACY E
      DOUBLE PRECISION E,TERM,SUM
      REAL X
      TERM=X
      DO 20 I=3,100,2
      TERM=TERM*X**2/(I*(I-1))
      IF(TERM.LT.E)GO TO 30
      SUM=SUM+(-1**(I/2))*TERM
   20 CONTINUE
   30 SIN=SUM
      RETURN
      END
```

This program is a straightforward implementation of the Maclaurin series

$$\sin(x) = x - \frac{x^3}{3!} + \frac{x^5}{5!} - \cdots$$

Although large values of x will cause truncation errors long before convergence, it will work for small values of x.

At least it should, if properly programmed. But what is the value of SUM when it is first referenced inside the loop? A search shows that SUM has never been set to anything, so it begins as garbage and in most systems accumulates more garbage with each successive call. This oversight is readily corrected, *if it is detected*. How do we find it? We might run some sample cases and compare them with a table or with another sine routine. (The latter is better because it is faster and less prone to error.) The important thing, however, is to check, for a casual look at the output may not always reveal that something is amiss.

Make sure all variables are initialized before use.

101

It would be well to test this routine further, for it is still incorrect. Suppose X is negative upon entry, as it may often be. Then TERM is negative, and remains so after it is recomputed just inside the DO loop. So it will be less than E, and an immediate exit will take place. The "sine" computed, needless to say, is worthless. We replace the test by

```
IF (DABS(TERM) .LT. E) GOTO 30
```

and now we have a working sine routine.

Or do we?

Where there are two bugs, there is likely to be a third. Look at the clever expression used to provide alternating signs for successive terms:

```
(-1**(I/2))
```

Is this expression "minus one to an integer power," as desired, or "one to an integer power, with a minus sign in front," which is always minus one? We encountered a similar expression in Chapter 2 that happened to work right. This one happens to work wrong.

Additional parentheses should be used in either case to remove all ambiguity. Even better, the computation inside the DO loop should be rewritten as

```
IF (DABS(TERM) .LT. E) GOTO 30
TERM = -TERM * X**2 / FLOAT(I*(I-1))
SUM = SUM + TERM
```

and the whole issue is avoided. Notice that the new TERM is added to SUM as soon as it is computed, thus ensuring that each TERM computed is accumulated before the loop is exited. This corrects the fourth bug in the routine. We also test for convergence before computing TERM, to eliminate any possibility of underflow should X already be very small upon entrance. This corrects a *fifth* bug.

Surely there is a more orderly way to write a program in the first place. As we suggested in Chapter 3, pseudo-code is a great help, particularly when the target language (Fortran in this case) is less than ideally expressive. We write in our anonymous language

```
sin = x
term = x
i = 3
WHILE (i < 100 & abs(term) >= e)
    term = -term * x**2 / (i*(i-1))
    sin = sin + term
    i = i + 2
return
```

and then translate into Fortran:

```
       DOUBLE PRECISION FUNCTION SIN(X, E)
       DOUBLE PRECISION E, TERM, SUM
       REAL X
C
       SIN = X
       TERM = X
       DO 20 I = 3, 100, 2
          IF (DABS(TERM) .LT. E) GOTO 30
             TERM = -TERM * X**2 / FLOAT(I*(I-1))
             SIN = SIN + TERM
   20  CONTINUE
   30  RETURN
       END
```

In this case, the pseudo-code WHILE becomes a DO followed by an IF. The Fortran DO neatly summarizes the initialization, incrementing, and testing of I, and keeps the loop control separate from the computation. It is a useful statement. The important thing is to recognize its shortcomings and plan loops in terms of the more general WHILE.

Exercise: determine if we *now* have a working sine routine.

Don't stop at one bug.

Sometimes there are several initialization errors, as in this code:

```
C      CURRENT COMPUTING PROGRAM
C      INPUT VALUES FOR RESISTANCE,FREQUENCY AND INDUCTANCE
       READ(5,20) R,F,L
   20  FORMAT(3F10.4)
C      PRINT VALUES OF RESISTANCE,FREQUENCY AND INDUCTANCE
       WRITE(6,30) R,F,L
   30  FORMAT(3H1R=,F14.4,4H  F=,F14.4,4H  L=,F14.4)
C      INPUT STARTING AND TERMINATING VALUES OF CAPACITANCE,AND INCREMENT
       READ(5,40) SC,TC,CI
   40  FORMAT(3F10.6)
C      SET CAPACITANCE TO STARTING VALUE
       C=SC
C      SET VOLTAGE TO STARTING VALUE
       V=1.0
C      PRINT VALUE OF VOLTAGE
   50  WRITE(6,60) V
   60  FORMAT(3H0V=,F5.0)
C      COMPUTE CURRENT AI
   70  AI = E / SQRT(R**2 + (6.2832*F*L - 1.0/(6.2832*F*C))**2)
C      PRINT VALUES OF CAPACITANCE AND CURRENT
       WRITE(6,80) C,AI
   80  FORMAT(3H0C=,F7.5,4H  I=,F7.5)
C      INCREASE VALUE OF CAPACITANCE
       C = C + CI
       IF (C .LE. TC) GO TO 70
C      INCREASE VALUE OF VOLTAGE
       V = V + 1.0
C      STOP IF VOLTAGE IS GREATER THAN 3.0
       IF (V .LE. 3.0) GO TO 50
       STOP
       END
```

This program is thoroughly, even excessively, commented. Most of the input parameters are printed out for inspection and verification. But there are several errors that warrant discussion. To begin with, what is the value of E when statement 70 is executed? Again we must search through the code, to find that it has never been set.

On some computer systems, storage is initialized to zero at the beginning of a run; in such cases, this bug should come to light when it is observed that the current is zero for all values of C and V. But if storage is left at some random value, which is true on many systems, the current computed will be wrong (although it might look plausible).

Simple oversight is the most common way to botch initialization. It seems likely, however, that this particular error arose because the programmer was not clear in his mind whether voltage was V (a mnemonic) or E (common usage among electrical engineers, to whom this program is directed).

There are other troubles with this program. Since L is not declared REAL, it is an integer by default. What happens when an integer variable is read in and printed out with a floating point (F) format? We do not know for certain, but we can guess that it will not likely be what was wanted. The missing declaration for L also means that statement 70 contains a mixed-mode expression. If the version of Fortran in use accepts mixed mode, the line will be executed, but probably incorrectly, because it will use whatever has been placed in L as if it were an integer.

Most serious is the error in logic. The program prints the values of C and AI for a series of capacitances, while V is 1.0. Then when C exceeds TC, V is increased by 1.0 (to 2.0), and we return to statement 50. But C is never reinitialized to SC, so after printing *one* value of AI with V equal to 2.0, we immediately increment V to 3.0. We then print one more value of AI (again with C beyond TC), and stop.

It is improbable that this is what the program should do. C has not been initialized to SC each time that V is changed. Whenever you have to build a loop out of spare parts because a DO statement is not suitable, take pains to display clearly how the control parameters are initialized, incremented and tested:

```
      ...
C LOOP ON V
      V = 1.0
   50    WRITE(6,60) V
   60    FORMAT('0', 'VOLTAGE=', F5.0)
C LOOP ON C
      C = SC
   70    AI = V/SQRT(R**2 + (6.2832*F*L - 1.0/(6.2832*F*C))**2)
         WRITE(6,71) C, AI
   71    FORMAT('0', 'CAPACITANCE=', E16.5, '  CURRENT=', E16.5)
         C = C + CI
         IF (C .LE. TC) GOTO 70
      V = V + 1.0
      IF (V .LE. 3.0) GOTO 50
      STOP
      END
```

We will have more to say later in this chapter about the questionable wisdom of using a floating point increment like

```
        C = C + CI
```

to step through a set of values, but for the moment we will let it pass.

Finding initialization errors is difficult and time-consuming. If you have access to a compiler that checks whether variables have been set before being used (such as WATFIV, IBM's PL/I checkout compiler, PL/C, etc.) use it. Worrying about the "cost" of using a debugging compiler is false economy. Your time is worth more than the small amount of machine time involved. More to the point, you may not find out about some error until it is too late.

Use debugging compilers.

There is another type of faulty initialization which will not be detected by debugging compilers. It occurs regularly in code that uses Fortran's DATA statement to set values. Here is an excerpt from a program we have already seen in Chapter 5:

```
      INTEGER NAME,COLOR,LAST,COL(6),COUNT(6)
      DATA COL/3HBLA,3HBLU,3HBRO,3HGRE,3HRED,3HWHI/,
     1 LAST,COUNT/4H0000,6*0/
      . . .
```

Suppose this free-standing program is converted to a subroutine. If the programmer forgets to replace the DATA statement that initializes COUNT by executable code like

```
      DO 10 I = 1,6
         COUNT(I) = 0
   10 CONTINUE
```

the subroutine will fail when called a second time, because the old values will remain in COUNT. The rule is: as much as possible, use DATA for things that are truly constant, like the table of colors in the example; execute initializing code for variables, like counts and sums.

In PL/I, the INITIAL attribute re-initializes AUTOMATIC variables upon each invocation of a procedure, so the problem is less severe. But you should still distinguish between true constants and initialized variables; declare them separately, and comment them clearly.

---

*Initialize constants with DATA statements or INITIAL attributes;
initialize variables with executable code.*

Another familiar class of errors is called "off-by-one": some action is done once too often or one time too few, because a test is botched or the limit of a loop is wrong. Let us look at some examples.

The following function sorts M numbers stored in the array V, by placing each number in turn in its correct position among the previous ones. (This is often called "insertion sorting.")

```
      SUBROUTINE SORT
      COMMON V, M
      REAL V(50)
      IF (M .LT. 2) GO TO 251
      DO 250 J = 1, M
        T = V(J + 1)
        DO 235 K = 1, J
          I = J + 1 - K
          IF (T .GE. V(I)) GO TO 245
          V(I + 1) = V(I)
235     CONTINUE
        I = 0
245     V(I + 1) = T
250     CONTINUE
251 CONTINUE
      RETURN
      END
```

The outer loop of SORT selects the next element to be inserted among the previous ones. Since there is no previous element for the first member of the array, it is somewhat surprising that the outer DO loop runs from 1 to M instead of 2 to M or 1 to M−1.

As might be expected, this is an error: when J reaches M, T is set to the non-existent V(M+1) and that in turn is inserted somewhere in the array.

The error is a classic off-by-one: the loop is done once too often. Fortunately, it is easy to fix this one. The outer loop should be

```
      DO 250 J = 1, M−1
```

Since Fortran does not permit the limit of a loop to be an expression, we must write instead

```
      M1 = M − 1
      DO 250 J = 1, M1
```

Watch out for off-by-one errors.

A common cause of off-by-one errors is an incorrect test, for example using "greater than" when "greater than or equal to" is actually needed. This program is a binary search routine, which looks for a particular element in a table by halving the interval in which the element might lie, until it ultimately either finds it, or deduces that it isn't present.

```
        LOW = 1;
        HIGH = LIMIT;                       /* LIMIT = TABLE SIZE */
    SEARCH_AGAIN:
        MID = (LOW + HIGH)/ 2;
        IF HIGH <= LOW THEN
          CALL ARG_NOT_FOUND;
        ELSE
          IF SEARCH_ARG = TABLE(MID) THEN
            CALL PROCESS_TABLE_FUNCTION;
          ELSE
            DO;
              IF SEARCH_ARG > TABLE(MID) THEN
                LOW = MID + 1;
              ELSE
                HIGH = MID - 1;
              GO TO SEARCH_AGAIN;
            END;
```

We will be talking more about binary search shortly, but for now, observe that if the table contains only one entry, then HIGH and LOW are both 1, and so the routine decides that the desired value, SEARCH_ARG, is not in the table without ever looking at either value or table! The problem, of course, is that the "<=" should be "<". (As an exercise, find the other cases for which this code fails.)

Take care to branch the right way on equality.

Here is another instance where branching the wrong way on equality results in a small but real error. The code computes a table of monthly balances and interest charges for a given principal amount, interest rate, and monthly payment.

```
DECLARE (A,R,M,B,C,P)   FIXED DECIMAL (13,4);

L10:GET LIST (A,R,M);
    PUT EDIT ('THE AMOUNT IS',A)(A(13),F(10,2))
             ('    THE INTEREST RATE IS',R)(A(23),F(6,21))
             ('    THE MONTHLY PAYMENT IS',M)(A(25),F(8,2));
    IF M<=A*R/1200 THEN GO TO L30;
    PUT SKIP(3)EDIT
('          MONTH        BALANCE    CHARGE        PAID ON PRINCIPAL')(A);
    PUT SKIP;
    B=A;
DO I=1 TO 60;
  C=B*R/1200;
  IF B+C<M THEN GO TO L20;
  P=M-C;   B=B-P;
  PUT SKIP EDIT (I,B,C,P)(F(13),3 F(13,2));
END;
L20:PUT SKIP(2)EDIT ('THERE WILL BE A LAST PAYMENT OF:',B+C)
                                        (A(35),F(8,2));
    GO TO L10;
L30:PUT SKIP(2)EDIT ('UNACCEPTABLE MONTHLY PAYMENT')(A);
    GO TO L10;
```

What happens if the amounts are such that the balance due plus the interest charge

(B+C) just happens to equal the monthly payment M (within one-half cent)? The program takes an extra trip around the loop, recomputes B and C, and informs the user that "THERE WILL BE A LAST PAYMENT OF: 0.00". This is graceless.

We can patch the code to read

```
IF B+C < 0.005 THEN GOTO L10; /* FINAL PAYMENT ALREADY MADE */
IF B+C < M THEN GOTO L20;
```

but it would be better to reorganize it completely, so that it reads from top to bottom instead of branching about.

There is also an instance here of a familiar error. Notice that there are two exits from the DO loop, one from the side and one from the bottom, that arrive at the same place. This should always arouse suspicion. The program is designed to exit from the side when the loan is paid off with sixty payments or fewer, and from the bottom when it is not. What happens if it does exit from the bottom? The final payment is B+C, but although B has been recomputed to be the correct remaining balance, C is not recomputed before being used — it is the interest charge left over from the previous payment. Clearly the interest charge should be either zero, or recomputed from the new B, depending on whether the final payment is made immediately or after another month.

In either case, this is an error. (It must be coincidental that it is in the bank's favor.) Our version avoids this problem with the safer DO-WHILE construction. As we repair the code we can correct the illegal $F(6,21)$ format item in the first PUT statement, add a SKIP so the headings are placed on a new line instead of being tacked onto the end of whatever message was printed previously, and eliminate the unnecessary variable B and the poorly-named labels.

```
DECLARE (A, R, M, C, P) FIXED DECIMAL(13,4);
DECLARE TRUE BIT(1) INITIAL ('1'B);

DO WHILE (TRUE);
   GET LIST (A, R, M);
   PUT SKIP(3) EDIT ('THE AMOUNT IS', A) (A, F(10,2))
      ('   THE INTEREST RATE IS', R) (A, F(6,2))
      ('   THE MONTHLY PAYMENT IS', M) (A, F(8,2));
   C = A*R/1200;
   IF C >= M THEN
      PUT SKIP(2) EDIT ('UNACCEPTABLE MONTHLY PAYMENT') (A);
   ELSE DO;
      PUT SKIP(3) EDIT
         ('MONTH', 'BALANCE', 'CHARGE', 'PAID ON PRINCIPAL')
         (X(8), A, X(6), A, X(7), A, X(3), A);
      PUT SKIP;
      DO I = 1 TO 60 WHILE (A+C >= M);
         P = M - C;
         A = A - P;
         PUT SKIP EDIT (I, A, C, P) (F(13), 3 F(13,2));
         C = A*R/1200;
      END;
      IF A+C >= 0.005 THEN
         PUT SKIP(2) EDIT ('THERE WILL BE A LAST PAYMENT OF:', A+C)
            (A, X(5), F(10,2));
   END;
END;
```

We have now combined the separate loop exits into one, which ensures that the exit conditions will all be consistent. The interest charge C is now up-to-date whenever it might be needed. And bringing the tests together at the top keeps the program from doing anything inside the loop if there is nothing to do, so silly messages are avoided.

Avoid multiple exits from loops.

Here is another example of a common error. The program is another binary search procedure to find out where in a sorted table X an element A lies. If the table contains an entry that matches A, both of the indices LOW and IHIGH should point to that value; otherwise LOW and IHIGH should be the indices of the two table elements immediately below and above the input value A. The elements of the array X are already sorted into increasing order.

```
      DIMENSION X(200),Y(200)
      READ 50, N
   50 FORMAT(I5)
    2 READ 51, (X(K), Y(K), K = 1, N)
   51 FORMAT (2F10.5)
      READ 52,A
   52 FORMAT (F10.5)
      IF (X(1)-A)41, 41, 11
   41 IF(A-X(N))5, 5, 11
   11 PRINT 53,A
   53 FORMAT(1H ,F10.5,
    1       26H IS NOT IN RANGE OF TABLE.)
      STOP
    5 LOW = 1
      IHIGH = N
    6 IF (IHIGH-LOW-1)7, 12, 7
   12 PRINT 54, XLOW, YLOW, A, XHIGH, YHIGH
   54 FORMAT(1H 5F10.5)
      STOP
    7 MID = (LOW + IHIGH)/2
      IF (A-X(MID))9, 9, 10
    9 IHIGH = MID
      GO TO 6
   10 LOW = MID
      GO TO 6
      END
```

First we correct statement 12 to refer to the arrays X and Y, with the appropriate subscripts X(LOW), X(IHIGH), and so on. Presumably this error arose from a careless transcription from mathematical notation to Fortran. The program does not check that N is in range, but it does test whether A is inside the table range, which is good.

What happens if we try to search a table containing only one entry? LOW and IHIGH are both set to one, so we immediately go to statement 7, which sets MID to one as well. Now, since A equals X(1) (A has been tested to be sure it is in the table), we branch to statement 9, where IHIGH is set to one (which does not change it!) and we return to statement 6. LOW and IHIGH are still both set to one, so we immediately go to statement 7.... This program is going to run for a long time.

The problem is that not all possible reasons for terminating the search loop were taken into account. We could patch up this bug with special handling when N is 1, but before we do, let us examine another case. Suppose that the table contains several entries, and that the entry at X(1) happens to match A. Then IHIGH and MID will steadily converge toward 1, while LOW remains at 1. When IHIGH gets to either 3 or 4, MID is set to 2; then since A is less than X(2), IHIGH is set to 2. Now IHIGH–LOW is 1, so the IF at statement 6 sends us to statement 12, and we exit. LOW and IHIGH are left pointing at X(1) and X(2) even though there is an exact match at X(1). We leave it to the reader to decide how pervasive this error is.

Patching is no substitute for rewriting:

```
      REAL X(200), Y(200)
      READ 21, N
   21 FORMAT(I5)
      IF (1.LE.N .AND. N.LE.200) GOTO 30
         PRINT 23, N
   23      FORMAT(1X, 'BAD INPUT COUNT:', I10)
         STOP
   30 READ 31, (X(I), Y(I), I=1,N)
   31    FORMAT(2F10.5)
      READ 31, A
      IF (A.GE.X(1) .AND. A.LE.X(N)) GOTO 40
         PRINT 33, A, X(1), X(N)
   33      FORMAT(1X, F10.5, ' IS OUT OF TABLE RANGE', 2F10.5)
         STOP
   40 LOW = 1
      IHIGH = N
   50 IF (IHIGH-LOW .LE. 1) GOTO 60
         MID = (IHIGH+LOW)/2
         IF (A.LE.X(MID)) IHIGH = MID
         IF (A.GE.X(MID)) LOW = MID
         GOTO 50
   60 IF (A.EQ.X(LOW)) IHIGH = LOW
      IF (A.EQ.X(IHIGH)) LOW = IHIGH
      PRINT 61, X(LOW), Y(LOW), A, X(IHIGH), Y(IHIGH)
   61    FORMAT(1X, 5F10.5)
      STOP
      END
```

Our search loop is a DO-WHILE (while IHIGH−LOW>1) that can, under some circumstances, be performed *zero* times. Degenerate cases frequently arise where a piece of code has nothing to do — in this instance, when N is one or two, no search is necessary. In such cases it is important to "do nothing" gracefully; the DO-WHILE has this useful property.

Make sure your code "does nothing" gracefully.

Fortran programmers should remember that with most Fortran compilers the DO loop is always done once, regardless of its limits; an explicit test is necessary to "do" it zero times. For example, the subroutine INSERT inserts VALUE in the array V at position J. The current size of V is N; INSERT increments this after inserting VALUE.

```
      SUBROUTINE INSERT (V, N, J, VALUE)
      DIMENSION V(80)
      DO 10 I = J, N
         K = N + J - I
         V(K + 1) = V(K)
   10    CONTINUE
      V(J) = VALUE
      N = N + 1
      RETURN
      END
```

It seems natural to assume that if J equals N+1, the new element will simply be added at the end. This is also convenient for entering the first element in an empty array, for which N is zero.

But the Fortran DO loop does us in. The loop is done once even if J exceeds N, so when N is zero, V(0) is accessed. The best solution is to protect the loop with an IF:

```
      IF (J .GT. N) GOTO 20
          DO 10 I = J, N
              K = N + J - I
              V(K + 1) = V(K)
   10         CONTINUE
   20  V(J) = VALUE
       N = N + 1
```

The PL/I DO loop behaves more suitably; it guarantees that if the termination condition is already met when the DO is begun, the body of the loop is executed zero times. Precautions like the following are unnecessary:

```
J=1; IF F1=1 THEN GO TO L2;
 L1: DO I=1 TO F1-1; PUT SKIP LIST(I,PRICE(I)); END;
 L2: DO I=F1 TO F2; TEMP=ROUND(PRICE(I)*(1-.01*DISCNT(J)),2);
        PUT SKIP LIST(I,TEMP);   J=J+1;
        END;
IF F2=32 THEN GO TO OTL;
 L3: DO I=F2+1 TO 32; PUT SKIP LIST(I,PRICE(I)); END;
GO TO OTL;
```

The extra tests and branches add no safety factor. Quite the contrary, their existence makes the program that much harder to read and understand. The code will perform identically if the redundant tests are eliminated.

```
J = 1;
DO I = 1 TO F1-1;
    PUT SKIP LIST(I, PRICE(I));
END;
DO I = F1 TO F2;
    PUT SKIP LIST(I, ROUND(PRICE(I)*(1 - 0.01*DISCNT(J)),2));
    J = J + 1;
END;
DO I = F2+1 TO 32;
    PUT SKIP LIST(I, PRICE(I));
END;
GOTO OTL;
```

The revised version appears bigger only because we have used white space more generously; it actually has fewer statements.

How can a conscientious programmer avoid errors like those we have shown? How can code be tested to exterminate those that do creep in? Many of our examples have illustrated what might be called "boundary-condition" errors, errors that arise at a critical data value or decision region. Things go wrong only there, not for the vast majority of cases "in the middle."

So it seems likely that one good strategy, both for writing and for testing, is to concentrate on the boundaries inherent in the program. For example, in the binary search above, we might guess that since the search is based on powers of two, reasonable places to look for bugs are where N is 2^k, 2^k-1, and 2^k+1. Of course one boundary is always the trivial or null case, here when N equals one. And we hit the jackpot.

But by now we should have learned to be suspicious: where one bug is found, there may be an infestation. So we looked at another boundary, the case where the table contained a match for the input entry. And again we hit the jackpot.

For practice, let us examine the boundaries of the following routine, which computes the mean of a set of numbers.

```
      DIMENSION X(201)
      READ (5, 100) TEST
  100 FORMAT (F10.0)
C INITIALIZE
      SUM = 0.0
      COUNT = 0.0
C ADVANCE COUNTER ON EACH RETURN TO THIS POINT
    4 COUNT = COUNT + 1.0
      I = COUNT
C READ A DATA ITEM
      READ (5, 100) X(I)
C CHECK FOR END-OF-DECK SENTINEL
      IF (X(I) .EQ. TEST) GO TO 9
C PROCESS THE ITEM
      SUM = SUM + X(I)
      GO TO 4
C COMPUTE THE MEAN
    9 AVG = SUM / COUNT
      . . .
```

The value TEST is read first; the next occurrence of this value signals the end of the input.

The most obvious boundary in any program, and often the easiest to test, is what it does when presented with no data at all. So what happens if we try to find the average of zero items?

Rather surprisingly, the program does not attempt to divide by zero (which is good), yet the very fact that it divides by 1 instead of zero is suspicious, since no special precautions were taken. The next boundary, also easy, is for one data item. And this time we see what is wrong. When there is one data item, the program divides the running sum by 2 instead of 1. From here it is easy to verify that COUNT, which counts the number of data items, is always 1 too high when the average is computed. The program is only asymptotically correct.

Dividing by COUNT−1 instead of COUNT is a quick fix (except when COUNT is 1) but it is usually wiser to rewrite than to patch, just to make sure that all the problems have been found and that the code is still clean. The root of the trouble here is that there are two counters, I and COUNT, yet only one thing to count, and the states of the counters have become confused. Programs often have redundant variables, perhaps for historical reasons, that serve only to add unnecessary complexity. Considerable energy can be spent just trying to keep them in phase. COUNT and I are both incremented *before* a new value is read in. This is done so the new value can be put into X(I) before testing if it is an end of file signal. Of course COUNT should only be incremented after the new value is known not to be an end of file signal. Interestingly enough, the book from which this example is taken shows a flowchart with a correct solution, but in the process of going from flowchart to code, the increment of COUNT got moved to the wrong place. (The discrepancy between flowchart and code illustrates one of the problems of program documentation, a topic which we will study in Chapter 8.)

Rewriting in pseudo-code with only one counter leads to a neater solution:

```
read EOF test
sum = 0
i = 0
WHILE (get new value ¬= EOF)
   i = i + 1
   x(i) = new value
   sum = sum + new value
IF (i > 0)
   avg = sum / i
ELSE
   avg = 0
```

After we hand-test the pseudo-code at its boundaries, it can be translated into Fortran with some confidence in its correctness.

```
      REAL X(200)
      READ(5,100) TEST
100   FORMAT(F10.0)
      SUM = 0.0
      I = 0
10    READ(5,100) VAL
      IF (VAL .EQ. TEST) GOTO 20
         I = I + 1
         X(I) = VAL
         SUM = SUM + VAL
         GOTO 10
20    IF (I .GT. 0) AVG = SUM / FLOAT(I)
      IF (I .LE. 0) AVG = 0.0
      ...
```

As a small but satisfying sign of improvement, the array size needed to process 200 items is now 200 instead of 201, because the end of file signal is no longer stored in X.

Test programs at their boundary values.

Another way to head off potential disasters is to "program defensively." Anticipate that in spite of good intentions and careful checking, things will sometimes go awry, and take some steps to catch errors before they propagate too far. For example, here is a fragment of a checker-playing program — it counts the number of reds and blacks on the board. Reds are represented by $+1$, blacks by -1, and unoccupied squares by 0. There are no other legal values.

```
IF BOARD(I,J)=1 THEN REDS = REDS + 1 ;
IF BOARD(I,J)=-1 THEN BLACKS = BLACKS + 1 ;
```

Suppose we are debugging the code. In the best of all worlds, there would never be anything in BOARD(I,J) but legal values, but errors do happen. Therefore, use the fact that the cases of interest are disjoint, and write

```
IF BOARD(I, J) = 1 THEN
    REDS = REDS + 1;
ELSE IF BOARD(I, J) = -1 THEN
    BLACKS = BLACKS + 1;
ELSE IF BOARD(I, J) ¬= 0 THEN
    PUT SKIP LIST ('ILLEGAL PIECE:', I, J, BOARD(I,J));
```

If you ever get an ILLEGAL PIECE message, you have an early warning of some disastrous bug. At the cost of an occasional extra test and a little extra code, the program limits the spread of nonsense should anything damage the board.

Often a program can be made more resistant to errors at *no* additional cost:

```
GET LIST (N) ;
DO WHILE (N ¬= 0) ;
    GET LIST ((NUMBER(I) DO I = 1 TO N)) ;
    TOTAL = NUMBER(1) ;        /* INITIALIZE FOR SUM */
    DO I = 2 TO N ;
        TOTAL = TOTAL + NUMBER(I) ;
    END ;
    PUT LIST ((NUMBER(I) DO I = 1 TO N), TOTAL) ;
    GET LIST (N) ;
END ;
```

Presumably, the end of input is signaled by reading a zero value for N, so the DO-WHILE carefully tests for this case. Indeed it must, for otherwise the body of the loop will compute and print an incorrect TOTAL when N is zero. But the loop body will also behave incorrectly for negative N, and there is no protection against that.

Any arithmetic comparison can in principle yield three different results — less, equal, greater. Often only two outcomes are reasonable, the third being silly or "impossible." An important aspect of defensive programming is to be alert for these "impossible" conditions and to steer them in the safer direction (assuming the error is so impossible that it's not worth a special check and error message). In this case, the program is less vulnerable if we simply change the loop test to

```
DO WHILE (N > 0);
```

As a general rule, terminate a loop early if the impossible arises, so that infinite loops are avoided.

Program defensively.

Floating point arithmetic adds a new spectrum of errors, all based on the fact that the machine can represent numbers only to a finite precision. Here is a simple example, a program which integrates the polynomial x^2+2x+3 between the limits 1 and 10, by a trapezoidal approximation:

```
        AREA=0.
        X = 1.
        DELTX=0.1
9       Y=X**2+2.*X+3.
        X=X+DELTX
        YPLUS=X**2+2.*X+3.
10      AREA=AREA+(YPLUS+Y)/2.*DELTX
        IF(X-10.)9,15,15
15      WRITE(2,7)AREA
7       FORMAT(E20.8)
        STOP
        END
```

This should evaluate the function for X=1.0, 1.1, until X is 10.0, should it not? But try it, and you will discover that on many machines it in fact does an extra evaluation, the last one at X equal to 10.09999.... The reason is simple: "0.1" is not an exact fraction in a binary machine (in much the same way that 1/3 is not an exact fraction in a decimal world); its nearest representation in most machines happens to be slightly less than 0.1. Thus 10 times "0.1" is not 1.0000..., but is 0.9999..., and by extension, when "0.1" is added to 1.0 ninety times, the result is not 10.000..., but 9.999.... The test that terminates the loop is sensitive to the difference, and gives us an extra trip around.

The value of the integral is too high by over two percent for this function and range. This error could have been readily caught, since the function can be integrated by hand. The discrepancy might then have led to further analysis of the program. (People who worry about computing efficiency might also notice that the function is evaluated twice as often as it need be. Since the answers are wrong, however, this seems unimportant.)

The moral? Floating point numbers should never be used for counting. If you want intervals of 0.1, do it this way:

```
        AREA = 0.0
        X = 1.0
        Y = X**2 + 2.0*X + 3.0
        DELTX = 0.1
C                       STEPS OF 0.1 FROM 1.1 TO 10.0
        DO 10 I = 11,100
            X = FLOAT(I)/10.0
            YPLUS = X**2 + 2.0*X + 3.0
            AREA = AREA + DELTX*(YPLUS+Y)/2.0
            Y = YPLUS
10      CONTINUE
        WRITE(2,20) AREA
20      FORMAT(1PE20.8)
        STOP
        END
```

This also eliminates the redundant function evaluations.

10.0 times 0.1 is hardly ever 1.0.

As a spectacular example of what floating point errors can lead to, when compounded at a million instructions per second, let us look at these two programs, from consecutive pages of a text, each of which produces a table of natural logarithms:

```
Program 1:
  PUT EDIT ((LOG(A) DO A=1 TO 9.99 BY .01))(F(10,6));

Program 2:
  DECLARE A FIXED DECIMAL (4,2);

  DO A=1 TO 9.9 BY .1;
    PUT EDIT (A)(F(5,2));
    PUT EDIT ((LOG(A+B) DO B=0 TO .09 BY .01))(X(5),10 F(9,5));
  END;
```

We would hope that these produce identical tables, save for formatting. Since the text reproduces some of the output of these programs, let us show the values obtained for the logarithms of 3.00, 3.01, 3.02, 3.03:

```
Program 1:
  1.098563   1.101891   1.105208   1.108513  ...

Program 2:
  1.09861    1.10193    1.10525    1.10856  ...
```

A third of the way through the table, these differ by five parts in a hundred thousand, an uncomfortable error. Why are the answers so different? As a wise programmer once said, "Floating point numbers are like sandpiles: every time you move one, you lose a little sand and you pick up a little dirt." And after a few computations, things can get pretty dirty.

One of the first lessons that must be learned about floating point numbers is that tests for exact equality between two computed floating point numbers are almost certain to fail. For example,

```
C       RIGHT TRIANGLES
        LOGICAL RIGHT, DATA
        DO 1 K = 1,100
        READ (2,10) A, B, C
C       CHECK FOR NEGATIVE OR ZERO DATA
        DATA = A.GT.0. .AND. B.GT.0. .AND. C.GT.0.
        IF(.NOT.DATA) GO TO 2
C       CHECK FOR RIGHT-TRIANGLE CONDITION
        A = A**2
        B = B**2
        C = C**2
        RIGHT = A.EQ.B+C .OR. B.EQ.A+C .OR. C.EQ.A+B
1       WRITE(3,11) K, RIGHT
        CALL EXIT
C    ERROR MESSAGE
2       WRITE(1,12)
        STOP
10      FORMAT(3F10.4)
11      FORMAT(I6,L12)
12      FORMAT(11H DATA ERROR)
        END
```

The test for right triangles will fail on virtually all fractional values, because of truncation errors. For example, the triangle A=3.0, B=4.0, C=5.0 will be recognized as right-angled on most machines. But if we scale the values down by a factor of ten, the triangle A=0.3, B=0.4, C=0.5 will often not be "right-angled." The code has to be replaced by some criterion of "near enough." (And this must be relative, not absolute, as we saw in Chapter 1.)

We do not have space to go more deeply into the mysteries of floating point computation; that is the province of numerical analysts. We intend only to emphasize that floating point computations should be used cautiously when controlling an algorithm. They should seldom be used for counting, nor should two computed floating point values be compared only for equality.

Don't compare floating point numbers just for equality.

Let us summarize the main lessons of this chapter. Remember that the errors that we have shown are by no means all that can happen; they represent the common ones.

(1) Initialize variables before using them. Be sure that variables in subroutines and inner loops are properly reset between successive uses. Set constants at compile time and variables at run time. If a debugging compiler is available to check for initialization errors, use it.

(2) Watch for off-by-one errors. Be sure that things are done the right number of times, and that comparison tests branch the right way on equality.

(3) Check that array references do not go out of bounds. Again, if subscript-range checking is available from your compiler, use it.

(4) Avoid multiple exits from a loop. Keep exit tests close together and as near the top as possible.

(5) Test your program at its internal boundaries. This should be done before the program is run, and as a running check. Ask whether each loop might be performed zero times under some circumstances, and if you are writing in Fortran, augment DO statements with IF's if they may have to be skipped.

(6) Program defensively. Be aware of the kinds of things that could go wrong, and add code to check for them.

(7) Do not count with floating point numbers. Do not expect fractional floating point values to obey the familiar laws of arithmetic — they do not.

POINTS TO PONDER

6.1   This program is supposed to print $\sin(x)$ for $x=0$, 0.1, 0.2, ..., 1.0.   It actually contains several errors similar to some discussed in this chapter.   Find and fix them. Improve the style at the same time.

```
      X = 0.0
   10 SSIN = 0.0
      DO 20 I = 1, 100
      N = I - 1
      R = N
      TERM = -1.0**N*X**(2.0*R + 1.0)/(2.0*R+1.0)
      SSIN = SSIN + TERM
      IF (ABS(TERM) .LT. 0.00001) GO TO 30
   20 CONTINUE
   30 WRITE(6,40) X, SSIN
   40 FORMAT (F6.2, F14.8)
      X = X + 0.1
      IF (X .LE. 1.0) GO TO 10
      STOP
```

6.2   This program computes the mean of a set of numbers.   The end of the data is marked by a card containing a number greater than or equal to 99999.

```
  100    FORMAT(5F15.5)
         SUM = 0.
         DO 3 N = 1,5000
         READ(2,100) X
         IF (X - 99999.)3,4,4
  3      SUM = SUM + X
  4      XNUM = N - 1
         XMEAN = SUM/XNUM
         WRITE(3,100)XMEAN
```

The program "works for any number of data items up to 5000." True or false? (Hint: Try a couple of boundary conditions.)

6.3   We observed that one should never test floating point numbers for exact equality.   But here is one case where any rational person would believe that the comparison would work:

```
   95 N = N+1
      READ (5,100) DATA(N)
  100 FORMAT(F10.3)
      IF(DATA(N).NE.999.999) GO TO 95
```

If the input card contains 999.999 in the proper field, the program will stop reading, will it not?   Try this case and similar ones on your system.

On some systems, the routines in the compiler that convert "999.999" into its internal (binary) representation were written by different people than those who wrote the routines that convert "999.999" when a READ is executed.   Why are the routines not identical, since they perform the same function? (Answer: That is the state of the art of computing, and one of the reasons for this book.)

6.4   Now that you are alert to the perils of testing floating point numbers for equality, try fixing

```
C       FIRST ATTEMPT FOR APPROXIMATING AREA UNDER A CURVE
     1  AREA=0.0
        READ(2,10)T
    10  FORMAT(F10.4)
        H=0.1
        X=0.0
     2  XN=-X
        AREA=AREA+(6.0*(2.0**XN)+6.0*(2.0**(XN-H)))*0.1/2.0
        X=X+H
        IF(X-T)2,8,9
     8  WRITE(3,33)AREA
    33  FORMAT('AREA =',F8.5)
        GO TO 1
     9  CALL EXIT
        END
```

Do you think just changing the IF to

```
        IF (X-T) 2, 8, 8
```

is sufficient?

6.5   "Defensive programming" means anticipating problems in advance, and coding to avoid errors before they arise. What could you do to the following program fragments in the way of defensive programming?

(a)   This is the entire body of a procedure for computing the arcsine of X in degrees:

```
        IF X = 1 THEN RETURN(90);
        ELSE RETURN(ATAND(X/SQRT(1-X**2)));
```

(b)   This function finds the minimum element in an array A of N items.

```
        FUNCTION SMALL(A,N)
        DIMENSION A(1)
        SMALL = A(1)
        DO 1 K = 2,N
        IF(A(K) - SMALL)2,1,1
     2  SMALL = A(K)
     1  CONTINUE
        RETURN
        END
```

(c)   This is a PL/I table-search routine.

```
        I = 1;
        DO WHILE( I <= N & KEY ¬= TABLE.KEY(I) );
            I = I + 1;
        END;
        IF I <= N
            THEN DATA = TABLE.DATA(I);
            ELSE DATA = '';
```

(Hint: In what order are compound logical expressions evaluated by your local PL/I compiler?)

(d) This subroutine is supposed to rotate the rows of array B by one position (i.e.,
row 1 goes into row M, row 2 goes into row 1, ... and row M goes into row M–1).
The array C is used for temporary storage.

```
          SUBROUTINE ROTATE (B, M, N, C)
          DIMENSION B (M, N), C (N)
          DO 24 I = 1, N
          C (I) = B (M, I)
          B (M, I) = B (1, I)
   24     CONTINUE
          MM = M - 2
          DO 34 I = 1, MM
          DO 34 J = 1, N
          B (I, J) = B (I + 1, J)
   34     CONTINUE
          DO 44 I = 1, N
          B (M - 1, I) = C (I)
   44     CONTINUE
          RETURN
          END
```

Rewrite the subroutine so it rotates a column at a time instead of a row at a time.
Which is easier?

CHAPTER 7: EFFICIENCY AND INSTRUMENTATION

Machines have become increasingly cheap compared to people; any discussion of computer efficiency that fails to take this into account is shortsighted. "Efficiency" involves the reduction of overall cost — not just machine time over the life of the program, but also time spent by the programmer and by the users of the program.

A clean design is more easily modified as requirements change or as more is learned about what parts of the code consume significant amounts of execution time. A "clever" design that fails to work or to run fast enough can often be salvaged only at great cost. Efficiency does not have to be sacrificed in the interest of writing readable code — rather, writing readable code is often the only way to ensure efficient programs that are also easy to maintain and modify.

To begin, let us state the obvious. If a program doesn't work, it doesn't matter how fast it runs. For instance:

```
C       PAYROLL COMPUTATION PROGRAM
C       READ EMPLOYEES ID,HOURS WORKED AND PAY RATES
     10 READ(5,20) EMPID,HOURS,SRATE,ORATE
     20 FORMAT(2F5.0,2F5.2)
        IF(EMPID .EQ. 77777.0)GO TO 60
        IF(HOURS .GT. 40.0)GO TO 50
C       COMPUTE WEEKLY PAY
        WAGE = SRATE * HOURS
C       CONVERT EMPLOYEES ID TO FIXED POINT FOR PRINTOUT
        IEMPID = EMPID
C       PRINT EMPLOYEES ID AND WAGE
     30 WRITE(6,40) IEMPID,WAGE
     40 FORMAT(12H1EMPLOYEE ID,I5,7H   WAGE,F8.2)
        GO TO 10
C       COMPUTE OVERTIME PAY
     50 A = ORATE * (HOURS - 40.0)
C       COMPUTE BASE PAY
        B = SRATE * 40.0
C       COMPUTE TOTAL WAGE
        WAGE = A + B
        GO TO 30
     60 STOP
        END
```

After we unscramble the confusing flow of control, we can see that the integer version of the employee's ID, IEMPID, is not set correctly when there is overtime — its value is a leftover from the last employee who had no overtime. The cause is

123

trivial — `IEMPID` is not set immediately after input. A similar instance of this error appears in Chapter 5.

Disorganized code often leads to errors. One wonders if the excessively complicated structure of this program comes from an attempt to be "efficient." There are two distinct cases (overtime or not), with a different wage calculation for each. In order to test HOURS only once per employee, these cases are separated and then brought back together again incorrectly.

But if we test HOURS twice:

```
IF (HOURS .LE. 40.0) WAGE = SRATE * HOURS
IF (HOURS .GT. 40.0) WAGE = SRATE * 40.0 + ORATE*(HOURS-40.0)
```

indeed we do an extra test. But the program is simpler: two lines replace six, the unnecessary variables A and B disappear, and the logic flows directly from beginning to end. Not only is it now correct, but it can be seen to be correct.

Splitting the computation into two parts, only one of which is done, is preferred if each half requires a complicated calculation. But the code should still flow from top to bottom:

```
      IF (HOURS .GT. 40.0) GOTO 25
      standard calculation
      . . .
      GOTO 30
   25 overtime calculation
      . . .
   30 WRITE ...
```

in the standard Fortran implementation of an `IF-ELSE`.

Make it right before you make it faster.

The following program, which computes the bills for an electric company, is rather similar. The problem is specified as follows:

```
usage>500           bill = 14.50 + 0.025*(usage-500)
500>=usage>100      bill = 3.50 + 0.0275*(usage-100)
100>=usage>50       bill = 2.00 + 0.035*(usage-50)
else                bill = 2.00
```

In addition there is a discount for users of electric heat:

```
if heated by electricity, and
            usage<1000      no discount
            1000-10000      5%
            >10000          10%
```

The first version of the program is

```
/*-----FIRST COMPUTE THE BASIC BILL.-----***/
    IF USAGE > 500 THEN BILL = 14.50 + .025*(USAGE-500);
                ELSE IF USAGE > 50 THEN BILL = 2.00 + .035*(USAGE-50);
                            ELSE BILL = 2.00;

/***-----NOW APPLY THE DISCOUNT.-----***/
        IF HEAT
          THEN IF USAGE < 10000
                THEN IF USAGE > 1000 THEN BILL = BILL * .95;
                                ELSE;
                    ELSE BILL = BILL * .90;
```

To begin with, the case that deals with usage between 100 and 500 has been inadvertently left out. This is not a big problem, since the error works to the advantage of the electric company. There are also a couple of minor boundary errors, since the specification gives a 5% discount for the inclusive range 1000 to 10000, while the code gives it for the exclusive range. ("Take care to branch the right way on equality.")

The null ELSE (second to last line) handles the case where the usage is less than 1000; it is required because the decisions are made in the wrong order, as we discussed in Chapter 3.

Most interesting, however, is the second version of the program. The textbook says that "Since a customer with usage less than 500 will never receive a discount, the program will be more efficient if the test for the discount is made only when we already know the usage exceeds 500," and presents a more efficient version, as follows:

```
    IF USAGE > 500 THEN DO;
                    IF HEAT
                      THEN IF USAGE < 10000 THEN BILL = BILL * .95;
                                        ELSE;
                        ELSE BILL = BILL * .90;
                END;

        ELSE IF USAGE > 100THEN BILL = 3.50 + .0275*(USAGE-100);
                    ELSE IF USAGE > 50 THEN
                            BILL = 2.00+.035*(USAGE-50);
                            ELSE BILL=2.00;
```

As is often the case, the attempt at "efficiency" doesn't work out too well. Passing over the typo 100THEN, notice first that if USAGE exceeds 500, BILL is never initialized, so it is either a dreg from the previous customer or garbage. This oversight will probably be caught quickly once the program is actually run.

Less glaring, and therefore more likely to escape notice for a while, is the incorrect correspondence of IF's and ELSE's: the test

```
        IF HEAT
```

is paired with

```
        ELSE BILL = BILL * .90;
```

because the null ELSE wasn't removed during the modifications. Thus anyone whose usage is more than 500 but who *doesn't* heat with electricity gets a free 10% discount. One hopes that the increased efficiency of the program will help to compensate for giving everyone a 10% discount.

When logical conditions are as complicated as they are here, it is risky indeed to combine them. The whole thing should be separated into two stages, each doing its job in a proper order:

```
/* COMPUTE BASIC BILL */
IF USAGE > 500 THEN
    BILL = 14.50 + 0.025 * (USAGE-500);
ELSE IF USAGE > 100 THEN
    BILL = 3.50 + 0.0275 * (USAGE-100);
ELSE IF USAGE > 50 THEN
    BILL = 2.00 + 0.035 * (USAGE-50);
ELSE
    BILL = 2.00;

/* COMPUTE DISCOUNT FOR ELECTRIC HEAT */
IF HEAT & USAGE > 10000 THEN
    BILL = BILL * 0.90;
ELSE IF HEAT & USAGE >= 1000 THEN
    BILL = BILL * 0.95;
```

Concern for efficiency should be tempered with some concern for the probable benefits, and the probable costs.

Keep it right when you make it faster.

Here is another example, which replaces the first N elements of the array A by their factorials:

```
      SUBROUTINE ARRFAC (A,N)
      DIMENSION A(100)
      INTEGER A
      DO 2 I=1,N
      IF (A(I))2,2,4
C         FACTORIAL PROGRAM
    4 K=A(I)
      NFACT=1
      IF(K.EQ.1) GO TO 8
      DO 6 J=2,K
    6 NFACT=NFACT*J
    8 A(I)=NFACT
    2 CONTINUE
      RETURN
      END
```

Special handling is given the case where K (alias A(I)) equals one (but why doesn't the test branch to statement 2 instead of to 8?). Certainly the code runs slightly faster if K is 1, but the program is more involved. Remove the test, change the inner DO limits to J=1,K, eliminate the temporary variable NFACT, and the program still works well. Of course, it would be better if zero factorial were properly computed (it equals one), instead of being skipped as an error. At the same time it's easy to ensure that negative values are handled plausibly.

```
      SUBROUTINE ARRFAC(A, N)
      INTEGER A(N)
      DO 20 I = 1, N
         K = MAX0(A(I), 1)
         A(I) = 1
         DO 10 J = 1, K
            A(I) = A(I) * J
 10      CONTINUE
 20   CONTINUE
      RETURN
      END
```

If the utmost in speed were of any importance here, the way to get it is obviously not to test whether K is one, but to pre-compute a table of factorials, and index into that directly. The table will not be very big on any current computer, since the factorials rapidly get too large to store as exact integers. We have remarked several times that a change in data representation often simplifies control structure more profoundly than any amount of tweaking. Efficiency likewise depends strongly on data representation.

Make it clear before you make it faster.

This brings us to another important point: simplicity and clarity are often of more value than the microseconds possibly saved by clever coding. For instance, one text suggests that the loop

```
      DO 4 J = 1,1000
 4    X(J) = J
```

be replaced by

```
      Z = 0.0
      DO 4 J = 1,1000
      Z = Z + 1.0
 4    X(J) = Z
```

presumably to avoid a thousand conversions to floating point.

This is an excellent example of nit-picking. One compiler we tried compiled the first loop into nine machine instructions, the second loop into eight. If all instructions were to take about the same time, the time saving would be a little over ten per cent. If this loop is ten per cent of an entire program (which seems high, since it is clearly just an initialization), the "improved" program would run one percent faster. As a matter of fact, the "improved" code uses a higher proportion of floating point instructions, which are more time consuming, so any saving is debatable. A second compiler *increased* the number of instructions for the "improved" version from ten to eleven, making the program slower! Trivia rarely affect efficiency. Are all the machinations worth it, when their primary effect is to make the code less readable?

Don't sacrifice clarity for small gains in "efficiency."

Sometimes a preoccupation with minutiae lets obvious things slip by unnoticed. In the code

```
I = K + 1
DO 6 J = 1,30
6 A(J) = B(J) * C(I)
```

one text observes correctly that C(I) is a constant within the loop, and thus there is no need to make the subscript computation repeatedly. The suggested remedy is

```
I = K + 1
TEMP = C(I)
DO 6 J = 1,30
6 A(J) = B(J) * TEMP
```

Many compilers will do the trivial optimization of moving constants out of a loop without being asked. (By knowing too much, you may even impede their efforts.) But even for a simple-minded compiler, the first two lines should certainly be combined into

```
TEMP = C(K+1)
```

Let your compiler do the simple optimizations.

The attempt to re-use pieces of code often leads to tightly knotted programs, difficult to get right, to understand, and to modify later, as in this program that decides if a number is prime:

```
ST1: GET LIST(N);
  IF N¬>1 THEN
    PUT EDIT('ILLEGAL INPUT N=',N,' <= 1')(SKIP,X(10),A,F(5),A);
  ELSE DO; IF N<=3 THEN GO TO APRIME;
    IF N=2*FLOOR(N/2) THEN  NOPRIME: PUT EDIT(N,' IS NOT A PRIME ',
        'NUMBER')(SKIP,F(15),2 A);
    ELSE DO; DO R=3 TO SQRT(N) BY 2; IF N=R*FLOOR(N/R) THEN
        GO TO NOPRIME; END /* OF DO LOOP */;
  APRIME: PUT EDIT(N,' IS A PRIME NUMBER')(SKIP,F(15),A); END; END;
    GO TO ST1;
```

The dilemma seems to have been how to avoid duplicating the PUT statement that reports non-primes. The resulting code is almost unreadable. (This is partly the fault of its layout, which we will comment on in Chapter 8.) For instance, it contains a transfer from within an ELSE to the beginning of the corresponding THEN! And instead of using the MOD function to test divisibility, it simulates Fortran's truncating division with the FLOOR function. The code cries out for revision:

```
DECLARE (N, R) FIXED BINARY(31);
DECLARE YES BIT(1) INITIAL ('1'B), NO BIT(1) INITIAL ('0'B);
DECLARE PRIME BIT(1);

DO WHILE (YES);
   GET LIST(N);
   IF N <= 1 THEN
      PUT EDIT ('ILLEGAL INPUT N =', N, ' <= 1')
            (SKIP, X(10), A, F(5), A);
   ELSE DO;
      PRIME = YES;
      IF N > 2 & MOD(N, 2) = 0 THEN
         PRIME = NO;
      DO R = 3 TO SQRT(N) BY 2 WHILE (PRIME = YES);
         IF MOD(N, R) = 0 THEN
            PRIME = NO;
      END;
      IF PRIME THEN
         PUT EDIT (N, ' IS A PRIME NUMBER') (SKIP, F(15), A);
      ELSE
         PUT EDIT (N, ' IS NOT A PRIME NUMBER') (SKIP, F(15), A);
   END;
END;
```

This version is slightly longer, but markedly easier to understand. And it has no duplicated PUT statement either.

Don't strain to re-use code; reorganize instead.

A faster-running program is often the by-product of clear, straightforward code. As an example, this program computes $n!$ for $n = 3, 5, ..., 49$.

```
C FACTORIAL PROGRAM
      DOUBLE PRECISION FACTOR, X
      NAMELIST /OUT/I,FACTOR
      DO 100 I =3,50,2
      FACTOR = I
      J =I-1
      DO 200 K=1,J
      X=K
  200 FACTOR = FACTOR*X
  100 WRITE (6,OUT)
      STOP
      END
```

Admittedly one does not compute a table of odd factorials very often, but this program is needlessly complicated and wasteful, because it recomputes $n!$ from scratch for each n, instead of just multiplying the previous value by $n \times (n-1)$. Here's the simpler version:

```
      DOUBLE PRECISION FACTOR, X
      NAMELIST /OUT/ I, FACTOR
      FACTOR = 1.0D0
      DO 100 I = 3, 50, 2
         FACTOR = FACTOR * FLOAT(I*(I-1))
         WRITE(6,OUT)
  100 CONTINUE
      STOP
      END
```

Students of complexity theory will recognize that the first version requires computing time proportional to n^2; the second takes time proportional to n. The absolute amount of computer time saved in this specific case is obviously irrelevant, but the gain in intelligibility is significant.

The author of the factorial program, by the way, included some of the machine-generated answers from his program. The value of 3! is given as

```
      5.999999999999999
```

Other values, also integers, are printed just as badly. The I/O routines provided by this particular compiler (*not* by the textbook author) are a typical example of false economy (that is, misplaced efficiency), since they do not produce the most meaningful answer for the user. Not only did the routine distort what was almost certainly an exact floating point 6.0 in its haste, but it then decided (presumably) that it was "too inefficient" to round the decimal representation before printing it.

The Euclidean Algorithm computes the greatest common divisor of two integers KA and KB by a series of divisions. Here is part of a program to do it. (KA and KB are positive.)

```
      IF(KA-KB) 5, 5, 4
    4 KR = KA
      KA = KB
      KB = KR
    5 IF(KA) 6, 7, 6
    6 KR = KB - KB/KA*KA
      KB = KA
      KA = KR
      GO TO 5
    7 PRINT 102, KB
```

Mathematicians have grown used to assuming that KA is less than or equal to KB in the algorithm, and so when the program is implemented, the first four lines of code make sure this is the case. But a moment's reflection shows that if KA is greater than KB, the algorithm works anyway, since the first pass through the procedure does the reversal. Removing the explicit interchange shrinks the code by a factor of two, without increasing its complexity. At the same time we can use the MOD function to improve the readability:

```
  5 IF (KA .EQ. 0) GOTO 7
      KR = MOD(KB,KA)
      KB = KA
      KA = KR
      GOTO 5
  7 PRINT 102, KB
```

This is of course a DO-WHILE — the division is repeated while KA is not zero. And notice that it can be done zero times.

As another small instance of the same thing, consider

```
      DO 10 I=1,M
      IF(BP(I)+1.0)19,11,10
  11 IBN1(I) = BLNK
      IBN2(I) = BLNK
      GO TO 10
  19 BP(I) = -1.0
      IBN1(I) = BLNK
      IBN2(I) = BLNK
  10 CONTINUE
```

If BP(I) is less than or equal to −1, this excerpt will set BP(I) to −1 and put blanks in IBN1(I) and IBN2(I). The code uses a hard-to-read Fortran arithmetic IF that branches three ways, two almost-duplicated pieces of code, two extra labels and a GOTO, all to avoid setting BP(I) to −1 if it is already.

There is no need to make a special case. Write the code so it can be read:

```
      DO 10 I = 1, M
      IF (BP(I) .GT. -1.0) GOTO 10
          BP(I) = -1.0
          IBN1(I) = BLNK
          IBN2(I) = BLNK
  10 CONTINUE
```

Interestingly enough, our version will be more "efficient" on most machines, both in space and in time: although we may occasionally reset BP(I) unnecessarily, we do less bookkeeping. What did concern with "efficiency" in the original version produce, besides a bigger, slower, and more obscure program?

Make sure special cases are truly special.

Let us turn to sorting, an area where efficiency *is* important in practice. Here is an interchange sort:

```
      DIMENSION X(300)
C     READ NUMBERS TO BE SORTED.
      READ 1,N,(X(I),I=1,N)
    1 FORMAT(I3/(F5.1))
C     INITIALIZE TO MAKE N-1 COMPARISONS ON FIRST PASS.
      K=N-1
C     INITIALIZE TO BEGIN COMPARISONS WITH THE FIRST 2 NUMBERS.
    6 J=1
C     L IS USED TO RECORD THE FACT THAT AN INTERCHANGE OCCURS.
   19 L=0
C     MAKE COMPARISONS.
      DO 2 I=J,K
      IF(X(I)-X(I+1)) 2,2,3
C     AN INTERCHANGE IS TO TAKE PLACE.
C     IS THIS THE FIRST INTERCHANGE.
    3 IF(L) 20,21,20
C     RECORD POINT OF FIRST INTERCHANGE LESS ONE POSITION.
   21 J1=I-1
C     MAKE INTERCHANGE.
   20 SAVE=X(I)
      X(I)=X(I+1)
      X(I+1)=SAVE
C     RECORD POINT OF LAST INTERCHANGE (ACTUALLY ALL INTERCHANGES).
      L=I
    2 CONTINUE
C     DETERMINE IF NUMBERS ARE IN SEQUENCE.
      IF(L) 8,9,8
C     NUMBERS ARE NOT YET IN SEQUENCE.  SET DO PARAMETERS.
    8 K=L
C     DO NOT WANT TO START AT ZERO SO TEST J1 FOR VALUE OF 0.
      IF(J1) 6,6,7
    7 J=J1
      GO TO 19
    9 PRINT 16,N
      ... print numbers, etc.
```

In Chapter 5 we mentioned the perils of making the user specify the number of data points to be input rather than letting the machine do the counting. We have also discussed how this type of code fails when N is less than two. Similarly, we have often pointed out that arithmetic IF's are inadvisable, for they are less clear to the reader (Quickly! Does it sort up or down?), and always add the possibility of arithmetic overflow or underflow. And the hodge-podge of statement numbers makes it unnecessarily difficult to find one's way around the code.

But for now our primary subject is "efficiency." Inspection reveals that this sort program is carefully coded to squeeze most of the possible speed out of the basic algorithm. A switch L determines whether the table has been sorted in less than the maximum N-1 passes, so an early exit can be taken. The index J increases to skip over elements known to be already in order at the beginning of the array. The upper index K decreases over those in order at the end. The programmer has carefully avoided the trap of letting J become zero. And there are plenty of comments to explain what is going on. All in all, this should be a marked improvement over a basic no-bells-and-whistles version.

Let us put that hypothesis to the test, by constructing another sort program and comparing run times on identical data. Here is our interchange sort, absolutely devoid of frills. We do not even bother to eliminate comparisons between an element and itself.

```
      SUBROUTINE SORT(X, N)
C   SORT INCREASING, BY INTERCHANGE
      REAL X(N)
      IF (N .LT. 2) RETURN
      DO 20 I = 2, N
         DO 10 J = 1, I
            IF (X(I) .GE. X(J)) GOTO 10
               SAVE = X(I)
               X(I) = X(J)
               X(J) = SAVE
10       CONTINUE
20    CONTINUE
      RETURN
      END
```

This has about half as many lines of code as the "efficient" sort, and is simple enough that comments seem superfluous. We have coded it as a subroutine, a more likely usage. (Notice the immediate return if N is less than 2.)

How much faster is the "efficient" program than the simple-minded one? We eliminated the I/O statements from the former and made it into a subroutine, so we could directly compare sort times without I/O overhead. Then we sorted arrays of uniformly distributed random numbers (several arrays of each size). Here are some run times, in milliseconds:

size	"efficient"	simple	ratio
10	1	1	1.0
50	22	19	1.15
300	850	670	1.25
2000	38500	29200	1.3

As we might have anticipated, complexity again loses out to simplicity: not only has carefully-tailored code produced a 15 to 30 percent *increase* in run time, but the ratio appears to be getting worse as the size goes up.

Keep it simple to make it faster.

Although the simpler code is faster, it is still time-consuming for larger arrays — 30 seconds to sort 2000 numbers is extravagant *if it is done often.* (Done infrequently, it is probably irrelevant; the programmer time needed to make a noticeable improvement in speed is certainly more valuable than a few minutes of machine time.)

How can we really speed it up? Fundamental improvements in performance are most often made by algorithm changes, not by tuning. Let us demonstrate.

It is well known in the sorting business that the interchange sort is suitable only for sorting a handful of items. Here is a simple version of a better procedure, known as the Shell sort (after D. L. Shell). Conceptually it is similar to the "efficient" sort we began with, and certainly no more complicated.

The basic idea of the Shell sort is that in the early stages far-apart elements are compared, instead of adjacent ones. This tends to eliminate large amounts of disorder quickly, so later stages have less work to do. For each value of the interval between compared elements, if no exchanges have been made, the interval is decreased, until it reaches one, at which point it effectively becomes a simple interchange sort. If no exchanges are made when the interval is one, the data are sorted.

```
      SUBROUTINE SHELL(X, N)
      REAL X(N)
C   SORTS UP.  IF THERE ARE NO EXCHANGES (IEX=0) ON A SWEEP
C   THE COMPARISON GAP (IGAP) IS HALVED FOR THE NEXT SWEEP
      IGAP = N
    5 IF (IGAP .LE. 1) RETURN
      IGAP = IGAP/2
      IMAX = N-IGAP
   10    IEX = 0
         DO 20 I = 1,IMAX
            IPLUSG = I+IGAP
            IF (X(I) .LE. X(IPLUSG)) GOTO 20
               SAVE = X(I)
               X(I) = X(IPLUSG)
               X(IPLUSG) = SAVE
               IEX = 1
   20    CONTINUE
         IF (IEX .NE. 0) GOTO 10
      GOTO 5
      END
```

Here are the run time comparisons, in milliseconds:

size	"efficient"	simple	Shell
10	1	1	1.7
50	22	19	20
300	850	670	260
2000	38500	29200	3200

The run times speak for themselves — not only is the Shell sort faster by a factor of nine at 2000 elements, but the rate of increase is lower. (Be it noted that the Shell sort is *not* the fastest sort available; it is merely an easy step up from the usual interchange sorts.)

There are two lessons. First, time spent selecting a good algorithm is certain to pay larger dividends than time spent polishing an implementation of a poor method. Second, for any given algorithm, polishing is not likely to significantly improve a fundamentally sound, clean implementation. It may even make things worse.

Don't diddle code to make it faster — find a better algorithm.

Our conclusions about the sort programs are based on measurements, not on *a priori* notions of what will or will not be efficient. For example, theoretical studies predict that for large values of n, the Shell sort will be substantially faster than any interchange sort, for its run time grows as no more than $n^{1.5}$ instead of n^2. Common sense says that for small n, interchange sorts will be faster because they are simpler.

Neither theory nor common sense tells us where the cross-over takes place; that depends on programming. Measurements show that, for our particular programs, the transition takes place for n around 50, but that the disparity is not impractical even when n is 300.

These measurements are obtained by using a timing package to time a particular piece of code, like this:

```
CALL TICK(TIME)
code to be timed
CALL TICK(TIME)
```

TIME is set to the elapsed computation time since the last call to TICK, to whatever resolution the operating system provides. Most computer systems provide such a service. (An even better service, less commonly available, times each subroutine without any need to explicitly reference the timing package in the program being timed.)

Timing is not always sufficient. For example, precisely why is the simple sort faster than the "efficient" one? The real work of each is in comparisons and exchanges; the rest is bookkeeping. Could it be that the simple sort is faster because somehow it does much less real work, or does it just do less bookkeeping?

Instrumenting the program to make a simple measurement gives us the clue. We add two counters, NCOMP and NEXCH, to each program:

```
      . . .
C COUNT COMPARISONS
      NCOMP = NCOMP+1
      IF (X(I) .GE. X(J)) GOTO 10
C OUT OF ORDER; EXCHANGE AND COUNT
      NEXCH = NEXCH+1
      SAVE = X(I)
      . . .
```

The counters are initialized and printed outside the sort. Here are the results (including the Shell sort):

size	"efficient"	simple	Shell	
10	43	54	60	comparisons
	22	22	13	exchanges
50	1020	1280	880	
	570	570	150	
300	41000	45100	11500	
	22400	22400	1500	
2000	1920000	2000000	147000	
	1000000	1000000	18600	

The two interchange sorts do the same number of exchanges. But, although the "efficient" sort does fewer comparisons than the simple sort, the saving does not offset the cost of all the other operations. With some confidence we can conclude that the simple sort is faster because its bookkeeping is simpler. The Shell sort column shows conclusively why it is faster than the others for large n.

Beware of preconceptions about where a program spends its time. This avoids the error of looking in the wrong place for improvements. Of course, you have to have some working idea of which part of a program has the most effect on overall speed, but changes designed to improve efficiency should be based on solid measurement, not intuition.

A useful and cheap way to measure how a program spends its time is to count how many times each statement is executed. The resulting set of counts is called the program's "profile" (a term first used by D. E. Knuth in an article in *Software Practice and Experience,* April, 1971). Some enlightened computer centers make available a "profiler" to do this automatically for your program. It works by temporarily adding "N=N+1" statements to appropriate parts of the program.

Instrumentation such as counts, profiles, and subroutine timings helps you concentrate effort on those parts of the code which really need improvement. Although we have already obtained improvements without the aid of the profiler, we can illustrate its potential. Here is a program that collates grades, counting right and wrong answers for each student:

```
      ISUM=0
      DO 3 I=1,5
      IF(CORANS(I).EQ.STUANS(I))GO TO 4
      ICHECK(I)=0
      GO TO 30
   4  ICHECK(I)=1
      ISUM=ISUM+1
  30  IWRONG=5-ISUM
   3  CONTINUE
```

If we take the profile of this code, we observe that the statement

```
  30  IWRONG=5-ISUM
```

is executed five times for each student. Why is this necessary? Clearly the number of wrong answers need only be computed once, after we know how many were right (assuming there are no other possibilities).

The code contains a "performance bug" — although correct, it does more work than necessary, because of misplaced code. The statement should be outside the loop, with its label removed and the GO TO 30 changed to GOTO 3.

Instrument your programs.
Measure before making "efficiency" changes.

The cost of computing hardware has steadily decreased; software cost has steadily increased. "Efficiency" should concentrate on reducing the expensive parts of computing. To summarize the main points of this chapter.

(1) If a program is wrong, it doesn't matter how fast it is. Get it right before you start to "improve" it.

(2) Keep code clean and straightforward — don't try to make it fast while coding. Premature optimization is the root of all evil.

(3) Don't worry about optimizing every little calculation. Let the compiler do it for you.

(4) Worry about the algorithm, not about the details of code. Remember that data structure can profoundly affect how an algorithm must be implemented.

(5) Instrument a program during construction. Measure before deciding on "efficiency" changes. Leave the instrumentation in as the program evolves.

POINTS TO PONDER

7.1   In our local computer center, control cards must be in a fixed format: there must be a dollar-sign in column 1, the operation (e.g., "FORTRAN") begins in column 8, and any additional information begins in column 16. Any deviation in any card typically causes the run to be aborted. Fewer than 30,000 control cards are submitted per day.

(a) If processing free-form input were to add 100 microseconds per card of operating system overhead (a generous allowance), what would this flexibility cost per day? (Answer: 3 seconds.)

(b) What does it cost one user to have to re-submit one job because of a mispunched card?

(c) Debate the pros and cons of free-format versus fixed-format input from the users' and the system's viewpoints.

(d) Find some analogous examples of short-sighted economy at your computer center.

(e) [Term project] Try to get them changed.

7.2   Statement-frequency counts (profiles), although useful measurement tools in a simple language like Fortran, break down to some extent in more complex languages like PL/I where a single "statement" can involve substantial computation. (For example, consider the implicit array operations.) What kinds of Fortran statements require non-trivial amounts of computation? How could the compiler advise the user of the probable complexity of constructions in a program? Would it be worth it? What other aids can you suggest?

7.3   The table of comparisons and exchanges for the three sorts shows that the Shell sort has a much higher ratio of comparisons to exchanges than the interchange sorts. What does this imply? Can the information be used to improve the algorithm?

7.4   Our timing tests of sorting methods were made on arrays of random numbers. Experiment to decide what degree of non-randomness is necessary before the "efficient" sort is faster than the simple sort. What does non-randomness do to the Shell sort?

7.5   Recoding a program in assembly language to make it as fast as possible is a last resort usually taken too early and too often. There is a folk-theorem that "10 per cent of the code takes 90 percent of the run time." Develop a methodology for deciding what parts of a program should be converted to assembly language, based on this observation. (You might try to verify it first.)

7.6   The following program computes prime numbers by the Sieve of Eratosthenes:

```
L=10000;
BEGIN;
DECLARE N(L);
N=1; M=SQRT(L);
DO I=2 TO L;
   IF N(I)=0 THEN GO TO JUMP;
   PUT EDIT (I)(F(5));
   IF I<=M THEN DO K=I TO L/I;
      N(K*I)=0;
   END;
   JUMP:;
END;END;
```

Since two is the only even prime number, modify the program to test only two and odd numbers. (You should clean up the formatting and eliminate the label as you do.) Does your new version run twice as fast as the old? Nearly twice as fast? Measure and see.

   Modify the program to save storage by storing only odd numbers in the array N. What effect does this have on the run time?

CHAPTER 8: **DOCUMENTATION**

    The best documentation for a computer program is a clean structure. It also helps if the code is well formatted, with good mnemonic identifiers and labels (if any are needed), and a smattering of enlightening comments. Flowcharts and program descriptions are of secondary importance; the only reliable documentation of a computer program is the code itself. The reason is simple — whenever there are multiple representations of a program, the chance for discrepancy exists. If the code is in error, artistic flowcharts and detailed comments are to no avail. Only by reading the code can the programmer know for sure what the program does.

    This is not to say that programmers should never write documentation. Quite the contrary. In a project of any size it is vital to maintain readable descriptions of what each program is supposed to do, how it is used, how it interacts with other parts of the system, and on what principles it is based. These form useful guides to the code. What is *not* useful is a narrative description of what a given routine actually does on a line-by-line basis. Anything that contributes no new information, but merely echoes the code, is superfluous.

    If you write your code first in a pseudo-language, as we suggested in Chapter 3, then you already have an excellent "readable description of what each program is supposed to do." Keep the original around to refresh your memory when you have to alter the code — that way you won't have to "decompile" the actual program each time you want to figure out why you did something a certain way. If you include your pseudo-code as comments in your source code, you will in fact be helping everyone who must later read it.

    Although comments have no effect on code, of course, they are still physically a part of it, and thus provide most of program documentation. We will devote much of our attention to style in commenting.

    One thing we will *not* do is make pronouncements about how many comments a program should have. We have already seen examples that contain none and others with more comments than code. The right amount usually lies between these extremes, but an arbitrary rule, like "one comment for every three lines," is absurd.

    A comment is of zero (or negative) value if it is wrong. For example, in

```
C     TEST FOR NEGATIVE VALUE OF X.
      IF(XST) 5,5,3
      ...
    5 PRINT 11
   11 FORMAT(1H041HTHE VALUE OF X MUST BE GREATER THAN ZERO.)
```

the comment is certainly not correct, even assuming that X refers to XST. Fortunately this case is sufficiently obvious that it is not likely to mislead.

The more common situation is that the comment is correct but the code it describes is not:

```
      /* THIS TIME WE SHALL TEST FOR    */
      /* ODD NUMBERS.                   */
   IF MOD(X,2)=0 THEN
      DO; SUM = SUM + X;
      ODDNO = ODDNO + 1;
      END;
```

The comment tells us that we are testing for odd numbers, the name ODDNO encourages us to believe it, but the test still selects *even* numbers.

The trouble with comments that do not accurately reflect the code is that they may well be believed subconsciously, so the code itself is not examined critically. A programmer shaky in his understanding of the MOD function might accept this comment at face value, especially since the mnemonic identifier ODDNO provides confirmation. (To avoid this subconscious acceptance, in *The Psychology of Computer Programming* Weinberg suggests that comments should be written on the right side of the page and code on the left, so the comments can be *covered* during debugging.)

Make sure comments and code agree.

Comments should also convey new information:

```
C     NEXT TWO STATEMENTS TEST FOR XMAX, IF LESSTHAN 10**-8,GO TO 1000
C
      EPSI=1.E-8
      IF(XMAX.LE.EPSI) GO TO 1000
```

This contains the same boundary error we saw above — the branch on equality is not what the comment says it is. But even if the comment were true, it would be useless. A meaningful comment would explain the reason for the test instead of merely repeating it in words. Avoid empty remarks like

```
      K13 = K13 + 1;    /* INCREMENT COUNTER */
```

and

```
C     PRINT VALUE OF VOLTAGE
   50 WRITE(6,60) V
```

and

```
      ON ENDFILE(SYSIN) GO TO DATA_ERROR; /* TEST END-OF-FILE */
```

and

```
N1 = INDEX(TEXT,';');     /*INDEX OF ; IN STRING TEXT*/
NAME = SUBSTR(TEXT,1,N1-1);  /*SUBSTRING IN TEXT FROM 1 TO N1 MINUS1*/
N2 = LENGTH(NAME);        /*LENGTH OF STRING NAME*/
```

and

```
S = S + F * EXP (-(I*B/N)**2/8);
    /* S = S + F * E **(-(I * B/N) SQUARED/8 */
```

and

```
ILOOP: DO I = 1 /* BY +1 ASSUMED */ TO 2*N;
```

---

*Don't just echo the code with comments —
make every comment count.*

Comments should help the reader over the difficult spots in a program. But when a comment becomes too involved, ask whether the code itself is at fault. We have already seen, in Chapter 3,

```
DCL NEWIN DEC FLOAT (4);
    LARGE DEC FLOAT (4) INIT (.0E1);
/* .0 x 10**1 = .0 x 10 = 0.0                          */
```

where the comment "explains" the ill-considered initialization of LARGE. A bigger example is

```
/* WE NEED A LOOP TO PRINT    */
/* EACH LINE BECAUSE WE ARE   */
/* PRINTING COLUMNS AS ROWS.  */

DO J=1 TO 20;

PUT SKIP EDIT(COL(J),(THRUST(I,J)DO I = 1 TO
        10))(R(FORM));

FORM: FORMAT(X(5),A(9),X(4),10(X(4),F(7,1)));

/* WE CAN OMIT THE 'END'      */
/* STATEMENT FOR THIS LOOP    */
/* BECAUSE WE ARE ABOUT TO END */
/* THE PROCEDURE.             */
END CORRECT;
```

The first comment is incorrect, for we can certainly write

```
PUT EDIT ((COL(J), (THRUST(I,J) DO I = 1 TO 10) DO J = 1 TO 20))
    (SKIP, X(5), A(9), X(4), 10 (X(4), F(7,1)));
```

Since the format FORM appears only once in the program, we have moved it inside the PUT as well, en route adding the right parenthesis missing from the original.

The second comment uses four lines in place of the four characters

```
END;
```

Should the code be changed, the END will probably have to be added anyway.

Indeed the code is explained, probably for pedagogical reasons, but a bad practice well commented remains bad. (The last lines of the original maze program in Chapter 4 contain a similar instance.)

Another example where potentially dangerous code is treated with a comment instead of a rewrite is this fragment:

```
6 E=E+.5
C     TEST FOR VOLTAGE EXCEEDING 3.0.
      IF(E-3.01)5,7,7
```

Since the comment and the code disagree, something is afoot that we are not being told about. Why is the test against 3.01 instead of 3.0? The most likely explanation is that it defends against some form of floating point rounding error, but in the absence of a useful comment, we can only guess. The way to treat this situation is not by adding arbitrary unexplained tolerances to tests. If the code has to be this way, explain it, for it is certainly not obvious. But if (as seems more likely) it reflects a poor algorithm, *change the code.*

Don't comment bad code — rewrite it.

Variable names, labels, and even Fortran statement numbers can aid or hinder documentation. Well-chosen names jog the memory; too-similar or meaningless identifiers hamper understanding. For example:

```
LOGICAL EL,EM,EN,AKK,ELL,EMM,ENN,ELLL,EMMM,ENNN,ELLLL,EMMMM
...
EL = A.EQ.5.*C
EM = B.EQ.A+C
EN = C/B.EQ.C/A
AKK = A/B.EQ.B/C
ELL = A/B.EQ.C
EMM = B.LT.A
ENN = C.GT.B
ELLL = A.GT.C
EMMM = A.GE.B*C
ENNN = EM.OR.EN
ELLLL = EN.AND.AKK
EMMMM = .NOT.(EL.AND.EN)
PRINT 20,A,B,C,EL,EM,EN,AKK,ELL,EMM,ENN,ELLL,EMMM,ENNN,ELLLL,EMMMM
20 FORMAT (1X,3F10.1,12L5)
```

These names have no mnemonic significance — even AKK, although different from the others for no apparent reason, conveys no information. The similarities invite misunderstanding and typing errors.

One solution might be names reminiscent of the test performed, such as

```
BLTA = B .LT. A
```

but since this seems strained, it is probably easiest to make an array called E and put headings on the output. Then the FORMAT statement can serve as part of the documentation.

As another example, less artificial, consider the bowling score program that we rewrote in Chapter 3. That used identifiers like X, Y and L, which were devoid of mnemonic value. Here is the same program, this time with variable names chosen to indicate the function of the variable.

```
SCORE = 0;
BALL = 1;
DO FRAME = 1 TO 10;
   IF PINS(BALL) = 10 THEN DO;    /* STRIKE */
      SCORE = SCORE + 10 + PINS(BALL+1) + PINS(BALL+2);
      BALL = BALL + 1;
   END;
   ELSE IF PINS(BALL) + PINS(BALL+1) = 10 THEN DO;    /* SPARE */
      SCORE = SCORE + 10 + PINS(BALL+2);
      BALL = BALL + 2;
   END;
   ELSE DO;            /* REGULAR */
      SCORE = SCORE + PINS(BALL) + PINS(BALL+1);
      BALL = BALL + 2;
   END;
END;
RETURN(SCORE);
```

Which version would you rather have to figure out? Which version will be easier to change a year from now?

Use variable names that mean something.

Statement labels (in PL/I) or numbers (in Fortran) are "mnemonics" just as variable names are — they serve to aid the memory of the person reading the code. Make them meaningful. Look back at the "efficient" sort program of Chapter 7. The sequence of statement numbers in it was

        1, 6, 19, 3, 21, 20, 2, 8, 7, 9, 16, 17

When a statement in the middle of the code says

        GOTO 19

which way do you go? Fortran statement numbers should be used sparingly (avoid the arithmetic IF, which forces at least two upon you), and should be sequenced in increasing order, with gaps between for later insertions. In PL/I, statement labels are rarely needed, but when they are, make them descriptive of their function.

Use statement labels that mean something.

The physical layout of a program should also assist the reader (whether the original programmer or a later modifier) to understand the logical structure. In Chapter 7 we looked at

```
DECLARE (N,R)FIXED BINARY(31);   ON ENDFILE(SYSIN) GO TO EOJ;
  PUT EDIT('PRIME NUMBER RESULTS')(PAGE,X(13),A);
ST1: GET LIST(N);
  IF N¬>1 THEN
    PUT EDIT('ILLEGAL INPUT N=',N,' <= 1')(SKIP,X(10),A,F(5),A);
  ELSE DO; IF N<=3 THEN GO TO APRIME;
    IF N=2*FLOOR(N/2) THEN  NOPRIME: PUT EDIT(N,' IS NOT A PRIME ',
        'NUMBER')(SKIP,F(15),2 A);
      ELSE DO; DO R=3 TO SQRT(N) BY 2; IF N=R*FLOOR(N/R) THEN
        GO TO NOPRIME; END /* OF DO LOOP */;
  APRIME: PUT EDIT(N,' IS A PRIME NUMBER')(SKIP,F(15),A); END; END;
  GO TO ST1;
```

The attempt to squeeze the program into only a few lines has made it hard to read, and concealed the convolutions of the code. Try to find the label NOPRIME, and the executable statement on the same line as a declaration. In the construction

```
IF N¬>1 THEN
    PUT EDIT('ILLEGAL INPUT N=',N,' <= 1')(...)
```

why is the test written differently from the printed output? That makes it necessary to understand two things instead of one. Separating the semicolon from its statement in

```
END /* OF DO LOOP */;
```

although harmless enough here, is prone to error. Similarly the statement

```
                      PUT EDIT(N,' IS NOT A PRIME ',
    'NUMBER')(SKIP,F(15),2 A);
```

uses the card up to its right boundary to no purpose. The alphabetic string still has to be split onto the next card, which in turn demands the "2 A" format item. Put it all on one line. Our version of this program is in Chapter 7.

Format a program to help the reader understand it.

The single most important formatting convention that you can follow is to indent your programs properly, so the indentation conveys the structure of the program to the reader at a glance. Indentation must be done carefully, however, lest you confuse rather than enlighten.

```
IF CLOSE_BALANCE < 0 THEN SERV_CHARGE = 7.00;
   ELSE BEGIN;
   IF CLOSE_BALANCE < 100.00 THEN SERV_CHARGE = 2.00;
      ELSE BEGIN;
      IF LOW_BALANCE < 100.00 THEN SERV_CHARGE = 1.50;
         ELSE BEGIN;
         AVE_BALANCE = OPEN_BALANCE + HIGH_BALANCE +
                       LOW_BALANCE + CLOSE_BALANCE;
         IF AVE_BALANCE < 800 THEN SERV_CHARGE = 1.00;
            ELSE BEGIN;
            IF AVE_BALANCE < 1600 THEN SERV_CHARGE = 0.50;
            ELSE SERV_CHARGE = 0; END;
         END;
      END;
   END;
```

The indentation, though clearly systematic, is not a help. Nor do all the extraneous BEGIN-END pairs contribute much. If we eliminate the unnecessary grouping, and indent to show that the program is basically two CASE statements, things clarify remarkably.

```
IF CLOSE_BALANCE < 0 THEN
   SERV_CHARGE = 7.00;
ELSE IF CLOSE_BALANCE < 100.00 THEN
   SERV_CHARGE = 2.00;
ELSE IF LOW_BALANCE < 100.00 THEN
   SERV_CHARGE = 1.50;
ELSE DO;
   AVE_BALANCE = OPEN_BALANCE + HIGH_BALANCE +
      LOW_BALANCE + CLOSE_BALANCE;
   IF AVE_BALANCE < 800 THEN
      SERV_CHARGE = 1.00;
   ELSE IF AVE_BALANCE < 1600 THEN
      SERV_CHARGE = 0.50;
   ELSE
      SERV_CHARGE = 0;
END;
```

A CASE should *not* have each level of ELSE indented, as is often recommended. Placing all the ELSE-IF's of a CASE at one level makes the multi-way nature more clear, and also helps to keep long ones from disappearing off the right side of the page.

Indent to show the logical structure of a program.

Another example of how an ill-chosen layout can hinder comprehension is

```
IF A > B
   THEN S = 1;
   ELSE IF A = B
      THEN IF C > D
         THEN S = 2;
         ELSE S = 3;
      ELSE IF C > D
         THEN S = 4;
         ELSE IF C = D
            THEN S = 5;
            ELSE S = 6;
```

Again this is neatly indented to display the structure, but it doesn't help the reader to *understand*. Under what circumstances will S be assigned the value three? It is not easy to tell.

This code is almost in the form of a CASE statement. There is one violation: the case A=B has an IF-ELSE in its THEN clause. It is no surprise that this is the hardest part of the code to comprehend. So let us transform it accordingly:

```
IF A > B THEN
   S = 1;
ELSE IF A = B & C > D THEN
   S = 2;
ELSE IF A = B THEN
   S = 3;
ELSE IF C > D THEN
   S = 4;
ELSE IF C = D THEN
   S = 5;
ELSE
   S = 6;
```

At the cost of one additional comparison, we have obtained a familiar structure. Now we know for certain that one, and only one, case will be executed. Reading from the top down until the proper condition is met tells us which one.

The reader has undoubtedly noticed by now that our personal stylistic conventions for layout, comments, and the like are not absolutely uniform. Nonetheless, we have tried to be reasonably consistent, for unless we are consistent, you will not be able to count on what our formatting is trying to tell you about the programs. Good formatting is a part of good programming.

We conclude with a larger example of documentation. This program solves a set of N linear equations in N unknowns, using Gauss-Seidel iteration. Originally from a textbook, it appeared in an article entitled "How to Write a Readable Fortran Program," in *Datamation*, October, 1972.

```
C CASE STUDY 10
C THE GAUSS-SEIDEL METHOD FOR SOLVING SIMULTANEOUS EQUATIONS
C
C THE PROGRAM SOLVES A SYSTEM OF N EQUATIONS IN N UNKNOWNS.
C N MAY NOT EXCEED 80; N IS READ AS INPUT.
C ONLY THE NON-ZERO ELEMENTS NEED BE ENTERED, ONE ELEMENT PER DATA
C   CARD, WITH ROW AND COLUMN NUMBERS ON EACH CARD.
C A ROW NUMBER OF 99 ACTS AS AN END-OF-DATA SENTINEL.
C THE PROGRAM READS THE FOLLOWING PARAMETERS PRIOR TO ENTERING THE DATA
C   N -- THE NUMBER OF EQUATIONS IN THE SYSTEM FOR THIS RUN
C   MAXIT -- THE MAXIMUM NUMBER OF ITERATIONS TO BE PERMITTED
C   EPSLON -- THE CONVERGENCE CRITERION
C   BIGGST -- THE MAXIMUM SIZE (IN ABSOLUTE VALUE) TO BE PERMITTED
C      OF ANY COEFFICIENT OR CONSTANT TERM
C ALL INPUT IS CHECKED FOR VALIDITY, EVEN IF AN ERROR IS FOUND.
C
C
      DIMENSION A(80, 81), X(80)
      LOGICAL OK
C
C CLEAR ARRAYS
      DO 20 I = 1, 80
         X(I) = 0.0
         DO 10 J = 1, 81
            A(I, J) = 0.0
   10    CONTINUE
   20 CONTINUE
C
C READ CONTROL PARAMETERS DESCRIBED IN INTRODUCTORY COMMENTS
      READ (5, 100) N, MAXIT, EPSLON, BIGGST
      NPLUS1 = N + 1
C
C READ THE ELEMENTS OF THE ARRAYS, WITH CHECKING
C DO LOOP IS USED TO CONTROL MAXIMUM NUMBER OF ELEMENTS
C FIRST SET ERROR COUNT TO ZERO
      NERROR = 0
      LIMIT = N*NPLUS1 + 1
      DO 30 K = 1, LIMIT
         READ (5, 100) I, J, TEMP
         IF ( I .EQ. 99 ) GO TO 41
         OK = .TRUE.
         IF (      (I .LT. 1)
     1      .OR. (I .GT. N)
     2      .OR. (J .LT. 1)
     3      .OR. (J .GT. NPLUS1)
     4      .OR. (ABS(TEMP) .GT. BIGGST) ) OK = .FALSE.
         IF (      OK ) A(I, J) = TEMP
         IF ( .NOT. OK ) WRITE (6, 110) I, J, TEMP
         IF ( .NOT. OK ) NERROR = NERROR + 1
   30 CONTINUE
C
C IF DO IS SATISFIED, THERE WERE TOO MANY DATA CARDS FOR THE
C   VALUE OF N THAT WAS SPECIFIED -- WRITE ERROR COMMENT
      WRITE (6, 120)
      STOP
C
C ALL DATA CARDS HAVE BEEN READ -- CHECK ERROR COUNT AND STOP IF ANY
   41 IF ( NERROR .NE. 0 ) WRITE ( 6, 130) NERROR
      IF ( NERROR .NE. 0 ) STOP
C
C      BEGIN ITERATION SCHEME -- DO LOOP COUNTS THE NUMBER OF ITERATIONS
      DO 70 ITER = 1, MAXIT
C
C         ... NEXT STATEMENT IS EXECUTED ONCE PER SWEEP OF THE SYSTEM
         RESID = 0.0
C
C         ... INDEX I SELECTS A ROW
         DO 60 I = 1, N
C
C            ... NEXT STATEMENT IS EXECUTED ONCE PER ROW
            SUM = 0.0
C
C            ... GET SUM OF TERMS IN ROW I, NOT INCLUDING DIAGONAL TERM
            DO 50 J = 1, N
               IF ( J .NE. I ) SUM = SUM + A(I,J)*X(J)
```

```
      50       CONTINUE
C
C               ... COMPUTE THE NEW APPROXIMATION TO VARIABLE X(I)
                TEMP = (A(I, NPLUS1) - SUM) / A(I,I)
C
C               ... AT THE END OF A SWEEP OF ALL EQUATIONS, THE FOLLOWING
C               ... STATEMENT WILL HAVE PUT LARGEST RESIDUAL IN RESID
                IF (ABS(TEMP - X(I)) .GT. RESID ) RESID = ABS(TEMP - X(I))
C
C               ... STORE NEW APPROXIMATION TO VARIABLE X(I)
                X(I) = TEMP
      60       CONTINUE
C
C               ... ONE SWEEP HAS NOW BEEN COMPLETED --  PRINT VARIABLES
                WRITE (6, 140) (X(K), K = 1, N)
C
C               ... IF LARGEST RESIDUAL LESS THAN EPSLON, PROCESS HAS CONVERGED
                IF ( RESID .LT. EPSLON ) STOP
      70   CONTINUE
C
C IF THIS OUTER DO IS EVER SATISFIED, MORE THAN MAXIT ITERATIONS WOULD
C    BE NEEDED FOR CONVERGENCE -- WRITE ERROR COMMENT AND GIVE UP
          WRITE (6, 150) MAXIT
          STOP
C
C
 100   FORMAT (2I2, 2F10.0)
 110   FORMAT (1X, 'ERROR IN CARD WITH I = ',I2,', J = ',I2,
      1     ', VALUE = ', 1PE14.6)
 120   FORMAT ('0', 'DECK CONTAINED TOO MANY CARDS')
 130   FORMAT ('0', 'ERRORS FOUND IN ', I4, ' DATA CARDS - JOB ABORTED')
 140   FORMAT ('0', 8F12.5)
 150   FORMAT ('0', 'PROCESS DID NOT CONVERGE IN', I4, ' ITERATIONS')
       END
```

In almost every way, this is an excellent program. It validates its input data. It uses multiple loop exits to detect errors. In several places, the authors have sacrificed a tiny amount of computation time by re-testing a condition, to avoid extra labels and GOTO's.

And it is thoroughly commented and neatly formatted. Notice that even the data is commented. One of the most effective ways to document a program is simply to describe the data layout in detail. If you can specify for each important variable what values it can assume and how it gets changed, you have gone a long way to describing the program. (The checker-playing subroutine we looked at in Chapter 4 is another good example.)

Document your data layouts.

All in all, the code above is a model of programming style.

But there are a few difficulties. To begin with, what about modularity? When a single routine sprawls over several pages, it is hard to follow. Since well over half of the actual code is concerned with validating the data, this could profitably be made a separate input function, as we suggested in Chapters 4 and 5. Then the main program could read

```
      IF (INPUT(N, A, MAXIT, EPSLON) .EQ. ERROR) STOP
```

The modularization would have the advantage that each part of the program would fit comfortably on one page. (In fairness, we should observe that the textbook from which this program originally came had not yet introduced subroutines when the example was presented.)

And what about its readability? Here is a letter to the editor of *Datamation,* published shortly after the original article.

> In the October issue, [...] told us "How to Write a Readable Fortran Program." I wish they had followed their own advice in the example that they gave. Said example has so many comments in it that it is unreadable. I agree that program documentation is a long-neglected and important problem. And placing a comment card before each statement in a program *does* document it. It also makes the program unreadable. Grouping Fortran comments and program statements into logical blocks makes *both* of them readable with very little loss of clarity.
>
> Neal Paris
> Durham, North Carolina

Mr. Paris has a point. There are more comments than program; some of them convey little information. We use few comments in our programs — most of the programs are short enough to speak for themselves. And when a program cannot speak for itself, it is seldom the case that greater reliability or understanding will result by interposing yet another insulating layer of documentation between the code and reader.

Don't over-comment.

A second letter on the same subject also appeared in *Datamation:*

> The example given in the article, "How to Write a Readable Fortran Program" (Oct., p 73), illustrates one of the most common faults of comments in programs — that the comments don't agree with the program. The program itself illustrates one of the commonest programming mistakes — the failure to check controlling parameters for limits.
>
> Specifically, the last line of comment in the heading states reassuringly: "All input is checked for validity." So what happens? The very first READ statement reads four controlling parameters which are checked only by the field width in the format, not a very good way to do it. In particular, N is not checked for its limit of 80. The unchecked N is used to "check" the values of I and J. Hence, a too-large N may result in storing of data beyond the array bounds. The unchecked N also limits several DO loops in the program.
>
> N. M. Taylor
> Washington, D.C.

Ms. Taylor is also right. The comment, like the input checking, is slightly wrong.

As a final observation, not worth a letter to *Datamation,* try the program on the equations

```
      Y = 1.0
  X + Y = 2.0
```

The solution is obviously X=1.0, Y=1.0. What does the program do? Following the code, when I equals one in the first pass through the inner loop, we evaluate (one line after statement 50)

```
  TEMP = (A(I, NPLUS1) - SUM) / A(I,I)
```

But A(1,1) is zero, and the result is a division by zero.

The program, comments and formatting notwithstanding, fails on a significant class of equations — those which happen to have a zero on the diagonal. Of course, those familiar with the limitations of Gauss-Seidel iteration would know enough to avoid such cases, and the textbook contains a proper warning. But it is a small cost to add an extra test to detect a zero on the diagonal, however unlikely it may be.

Perhaps what the article really shows is that people who attempt to criticize programming style run the risk of being criticized in turn. On that note we bring our discussion to a close.

In summary:

(1) If a program is incorrect, it matters little what the documentation says.

(2) If documentation does not agree with the code, it is not worth much.

(3) Consequently, code must largely document itself. If it cannot, rewrite the code rather than increase the supplementary documentation. Good code needs fewer comments than bad code does.

(4) Comments should provide additional information that is not readily obtainable from the code itself. They should never parrot the code.

(5) Mnemonic variable names and labels, and a layout that emphasizes logical structure, help make a program self-documenting.

POINTS TO PONDER

8.1   Programming in a standard or stereotyped way is often a useful way to avoid error. For example, in Fortran, identifiers that begin with I, J, K, L, M, or N are integer by default, and all others are floating point. This convention is widely used. Sometimes, however, to avoid straining for meaningful identifiers, it seems easier to declare variables explicitly, overriding the default. From the standpoints of error potential and reader comprehension, is this good practice or bad? You might consider this excerpt in your deliberations:

```
C A SORTING PROGRAM
      ...
      INTEGER X, Y
      DIMENSION X(25), Y(25)
      ...
          IF ( X(I) .LE. X(J) ) GO TO 20
             TEMP = X(I)
             X(I) = X(J)
             X(J) = TEMP
             TEMP = Y(I)
             Y(I) = Y(J)
             Y(J) = TEMP
```

8.2   Fortran continuation lines are often left behind when statements are moved within a program. What practices can you think of, in writing multi-line statements, that would reduce the likelihood of your making this mistake (or at least ensure that the compiler will spot your error)? Look back over the Fortran programs in this book.

8.3   Comment on these comments:

```
      DO 65 L=1,9999
C        GENERATE RANDOM NUMBER
41    CALL RANDU(IX,IY,YFL)
C        SET NEW VALUE OF IX TO VALUE OF IY
      IX=IY
C        COMPUTE SAMPLE WHICH IS TO RECEIVE BACTERIA
      N=YFL*100.0 +1.0
C        CHECK TO SEE IF N IS 101
      IF(N-101) 40,41,40
C        CHECK TO SEE IF SAMPLE ALREADY CONTAINS BACTERIA
40    IF(IT(N) )21,20,21
C        INCREMENT NUMBER OF SAMPLES CONTAINING BACTERIA BY ONE
20    ICT=ICT+1
C        INCREMENT NUMBER OF BACTERIA IN SAMPLE BY ONE
21    IT(N)=IT(N)+1
C        CHECK TO SEE IF 50 OF THE SAMPLES CONTAIN BACTERIA
      IF(ICT-50)65,33,33
65    CONTINUE
```

EPILOGUE

It is time to take stock. Although we have touched on many aspects of computer programming in the last eight chapters, much has been left unsaid. In some cases this was due to lack of space, but most of the omissions were intentional. There are many good books on languages, algorithms and numerical methods available to those who want to learn programming in greater depth. Our goal was not to teach languages or algorithms, but to teach you to program well.

Programmers have a strong tendency to underrate the importance of good style. Eternally optimistic, we all like to think that once we throw a piece of code together, however haphazardly, it will work properly the first time and ever after. Why waste time cleaning up something that is almost certain to be correct? Besides, it probably will be used for only a few weeks.

There are really two answers to the question. The first is suggested by the word "almost." A slap-dash piece of code that falls short of perfection can be a difficult creature to deal with. The self-discipline of writing it cleanly the first time increases your chances of getting it right and eases the task of fixing it if it is not. The programmer who leaps to the coding pad or the terminal and throws a first draft at the machine spends far more time redoing and debugging than does his or her more careful colleague.

The second point is that phrase "only a few weeks." Certainly we write code differently depending on the ultimate use we expect to make of it. But computer centers are full of programs that were written for a short-term use, then were pressed into years of service. Not only pressed, but sometimes hammered and twisted. It is often simpler to modify existing code, no matter how badly written, than to reinvent the wheel yet again for a new application. Big programs — operating systems, compilers, major applications — are never written to be used once and discarded. They change and evolve. Most professional programmers spend much of their time *changing* their own and other people's code. We will say it once more — clean code is easier to maintain.

One excuse for writing an unintelligible program is that it is a private matter. Only the original programmer will ever look at it, and surely he need not spell out everything when he has it all in his head. This can be a strong argument, particularly if you don't program professionally. It is the same justification you use for writing "qt milk, fish, big box" for a grocery list instead of composing a proper sentence. If the list is intended for someone else, of course, you had better specify what kind of fish you want and what should be inside that big box. But even if only you personally want to understand the message, if it is to be readable a year from

155

now you must write a complete sentence. So in your diary you might write, "Today I went to the supermarket and bought a quart of milk, a pound of halibut, and a big box of raisins."

You learn to write as if to someone else because *next year you will be "someone else."* Schools teach English composition, not how to write grocery lists. The latter is easy once the former is mastered. Yet when it comes to computer programming, many programmers seem to think that a mastery of "grocery list" writing is adequate preparation for composing large programs. This is not so.

The essence of what we are trying to convey is summed up in the elusive word "style." It is not a list of rules so much as an approach and an attitude. "Good programmers" are those who already have learned a set of rules that ensures good style; many of them will read this book and see no reason to change. If you are still learning to be a "good programmer," however, then perhaps some of what we consider good style will have rubbed off in the reading.

SUPPLEMENTARY READING

F. P. Brooks, Jr., *The Mythical Man-Month.* Addison-Wesley, 1975.

O.-J. Dahl, E. W. Dijkstra, C. A. R. Hoare, *Structured Programming.* Academic Press, 1972.

Brian W. Kernighan and P. J. Plauger, *Software Tools,* Addison-Wesley, 1976.

W. Strunk, Jr., and E. B. White, *The Elements of Style.* MacMillan, 1972.

G. M. Weinberg, *The Psychology of Computer Programming.* Van Nostrand Reinhold, 1971.

SUMMARY OF RULES

This summary is designed to give a quick review of the points we covered in the book. Remember as you read the rules that they were presented in connection with one or more examples — go back and reread the pertinent section if a rule doesn't call them to mind.

To paraphrase an observation in *The Elements of Style,* rules of programming style, like those of English, are sometimes broken, even by the best writers. When a rule is broken, however, you will usually find in the program some compensating merit, attained at the cost of the violation. Unless you are certain of doing as well, you will probably do best to follow the rules.

Write clearly — don't be too clever.

Say what you mean, simply and directly.

Use library functions.

Avoid temporary variables.

Write clearly — don't sacrifice clarity for "efficiency."

Let the machine do the dirty work.

Replace repetitive expressions by calls to a common function.

Parenthesize to avoid ambiguity.

Choose variable names that won't be confused.

Avoid the Fortran arithmetic IF.

Avoid unnecessary branches.

Use the good features of a language; avoid the bad ones.

Don't use conditional branches as a substitute for a logical expression.

Use the "telephone test" for readability.

Use DO-END and indenting to delimit groups of statements.

Use IF-ELSE to emphasize that only one of two actions is to be performed.

Use DO and DO-WHILE to emphasize the presence of loops.

Make your programs read from top to bottom.

159

Use IF ... ELSE IF ... ELSE IF ... ELSE ... to implement multi-way branches.

Use the fundamental control flow constructs.

Write first in an easy-to-understand pseudo-language; then translate into whatever language you have to use.

Avoid THEN-IF and null ELSE.

Avoid ELSE GOTO and ELSE RETURN.

Follow each decision as closely as possible with its associated action.

Use data arrays to avoid repetitive control sequences.

Choose a data representation that makes the program simple.

Don't stop with your first draft.

Modularize.   Use subroutines.

Make the coupling between modules visible.

Each module should do one thing well.

Make sure every module hides something.

Let the data structure the program.

Don't patch bad code — rewrite it.

Write and test a big program in small pieces.

Use recursive procedures for recursively-defined data structures.

Test input for validity and plausibility.

Make sure input cannot violate the limits of the program.

Terminate input by end-of-file or marker, not by count.

Identify bad input; recover if possible.

Treat end of file conditions in a uniform manner.

Make input easy to prepare and output self-explanatory.

Use uniform input formats.

Make input easy to proofread.

Use free-form input when possible.

Use self-identifying input. Allow defaults. Echo both on output.

Localize input and output in subroutines.

Make sure all variables are initialized before use.

Don't stop at one bug.

Use debugging compilers.

Initialize constants with DATA statements or INITIAL attributes; initialize variables with executable code.

Watch out for off-by-one errors.

Take care to branch the right way on equality.

Avoid multiple exits from loops.

Make sure your code "does nothing" gracefully.

Test programs at their boundary values.

Program defensively.

10.0 times 0.1 is hardly ever 1.0.

Don't compare floating point numbers just for equality.

Make it right before you make it faster.

Keep it right when you make it faster.

Make it clear before you make it faster.

Don't sacrifice clarity for small gains in "efficiency."

Let your compiler do the simple optimizations.

Don't strain to re-use code; reorganize instead.

Make sure special cases are truly special.

Keep it simple to make it faster.

Don't diddle code to make it faster — find a better algorithm.

Instrument your programs. Measure before making "efficiency" changes.

Make sure comments and code agree.

Don't just echo the code with comments — make every comment count.

Don't comment bad code — rewrite it.

Use variable names that mean something.

Use statement labels that mean something.

Format a program to help the reader understand it.

Indent to show the logical structure of a program.

Document your data layouts.

Don't over-comment.